BUS STOP PRAYERS

Praying the Psalms
Over Your School-Aged Children

Lauren Golis

ISBN 978-1-64515-118-0 (paperback)
ISBN 978-1-64515-119-7 (digital)

Copyright © 2019 by Lauren Golis

All rights reserved. No part of this publication may be reproduced, distributed, or transmitted in any form or by any means, including photocopying, recording, or other electronic or mechanical methods without the prior written permission of the publisher. For permission requests, solicit the publisher via the address below.

Christian Faith Publishing, Inc.
832 Park Avenue
Meadville, PA 16335
www.christianfaithpublishing.com

All Bible verses are taken from the NIV translation.

Printed in the United States of America

"Let this be written, for a future generation, that a people not yet created may praise the Lord."

Psalm 102:18

BUS STOP PRAYERS

Dear Father,

It is my prayer and deepest desire for the Psalm-inspired prayers in this book to bring generations of children to love and walk with you each day. I pray these words, taken from your alive and holy Word, will change the lives of each child. May your divine influence be upon each child and caregiver every moment of every day. Ultimately, I pray each precious life will bring glory back to you. I lift up the children of the next generations to you, that they will not walk in darkness and cling to lies and worthless idols. Instead, let them seek your Truth and walk in the light of your Son, Jesus Christ, our Redeemer and Savior.

I pray for your good and perfect will to be done.

In Jesus's name,
Amen

Even before my children were born, I remember praying for them in the womb. I prayed passionately for each one to be blessed by God and be used by him to accomplish the kingdom work he had planned. It wasn't until a few months after my daughter was born, that I realized, while reading to her before her nap, I had a role to play in leading her to the Lord. God was showing me the need for daily exposure to him everywhere in her life as she was growing up. Most of all, I learned that I need to be constantly connected to him in order for his love, guidance, and strength to flow through me and into the lives of my children.

That faithful day when my daughter started kindergarten and was leaving the protection of our home and going out into the world, I was made aware of the spiritual battle going on around us every day. I longed to protect her and to lean on God's promise that he will always be with us wherever we go. I began praying for her at the bus stop before she left for school. After a few weeks, my prayers started to become redundant and I felt the Lord asking more of me in my prayers for her. That is when I turned to the Psalms for guidance. I loved reading each heartfelt, emotional verse and began using God's Word to pray for my children.

When I take the time to pray God's specific Word over my children, I can see his work in our lives more clearly and go about my day differently. I feel filled with his presence, ready to work for his purpose in my life and in the lives of our children. It also brings me peace to know they are covered in prayer and that ultimately God is in control. This parenting journey is filled with ups and downs, joy and pain, laughter and tears. God promises to be there beside us, guiding us to his will, giving us grace, hope, and a future. All we need to do is have a willing and faithful heart and stay connected to him in prayer.

I feel humbled by God's call to share this compilation of prayers from my heart with you, so your family may experience his blessing and presence. Most of all, I pray these prayers will lift up your children and your children's children to the Lord and they will one day ask Jesus to be their loving Savior. May his love be passed down from generation to generation.

In his love,
Lauren

"Blessed is the one who does not walk in step with the wicked or stand in the way that sinners take or sit in the company of mockers, but whose delight is in the law of the Lord, and who meditates on his law day and night. That person is like a tree planted by streams of water, which yields its fruit in season and whose leaf does not wither – whatever they do prospers."

Psalm 1:1–3

Dear God,

We rejoice in your name this morning! I lift up my children to you, that they will not walk in the ways of the wicked and stray from you. The thought of my children choosing anything but you breaks my heart. *May my children delight in your law, so they will be like a tree planted by streams of water, yielding its fruit in season Psalm 1:3 (NIV).* Thank you for being at work in their hearts, Father. I pray they will love you, your Son, and serve you throughout their entire lives. I can't do this without you.

In Jesus's name,
Amen

"But you, Lord, are a shield around me, my glory, the one who lifts my head high. I call out to the Lord, and he answers me from his holy mountain. I lie down and sleep; I wake again, because the Lord sustains me."

Psalm 3:3–5

Dear God,

    Thank you Father for the gift of this day! Each day we wake up because of your goodness. Only you know what today will bring. I call for your help, Father. I pray for my children to learn to look to you to sustain them today and every day. As they are at school, let your glory shine upon them so that others will see this beautiful light inside their heart. I give thanks each day that I can call on your name and Word for help in raising these beautiful children you gave me. Thank you for the answers to my prayers, in whatever form that is you choose. We love you, dear Father.
    In Jesus's name,
    Amen

*"…Let the light of your
face shine on us."*

Psalm 4:6

*"Lead me, Lord, in your
righteousness because of my
enemies—make your way
straight before me."*

Psalm 5:8

Dear God,

Let the light of your face shine upon my family this morning, o Lord. You hear our voices as we come to you with our requests and wait in expectation. I want what you want for my children this day. I leave my prayer open for you to fill with your immeasurable goodness. I pray our eyes will see and appreciate even the tiniest detail of your work today. Make straight your way before my children. Let them follow in your good and perfect will. Give them a heart of gladness so they will be able to sing for joy in you. Spread your protection over my children, as we rejoice in your holy name.

In Jesus's name,
Amen

"I will give thanks to the Lord because of his righteousness; I will sing the praises of the name of the Lord most high."

Psalm 7:17

"Lord, our Lord, how majestic is your name in all the earth!"

Psalm 8:1–9

Dear Lord,

As we rise this morning, we marvel at your creation! The rising sun makes everything sparkle as it is covered in a fresh white blanket of frost and snow. We humble ourselves in your presence, dear Lord. Thank you for caring for us each day, giving us love, joy, protection, mercy, grace, and forgiveness. Even though we are so small, you chose to crown us with your glory. May my children feel such joy in their hearts from you that they can't help but sing praises to your name all throughout their day today.

In Jesus's name,

Amen

"I will give thanks to you, Lord, with all my heart; I will tell of all your wonderful deeds."

Psalm 9:1

"The Lord is a refuge for the oppressed, a stronghold in times of trouble. Those who know your name trust in you, for you, Lord, have never forsaken those who seek you. Sing the praises of the Lord, enthroned in Zion; proclaim among the nations what he has done."

Psalm 9:9–11

BUS STOP PRAYERS

Dear God,

We praise you Father with all our heart. Help me to tell of your wonders to my children and for them to have the strength and courage to tell of your wonders to others they meet. Make our hearts glad as we rejoice in you in all that we do today. We place our trust in you this day, and every day, for your Word says *the Lord has never forsaken those who seek him Psalm 9:10 (NIV)*. I pray my children will remember to trust you as their refuge when they are faced with troubles.

In Jesus's name,
Amen

*"But I trust in your unfailing love;
my heart rejoices in your salvation.
I will sing the Lord's praise,
for he has been good to me."*

Psalm 13:5–6

*"Keep me safe, my God, for in you
I take refuge. I say to the Lord,
'You are my Lord; apart from you
I have no good thing.'… You make
known to me the path of life…"*

Psalm 16:1–2, 11

BUS STOP PRAYERS

Dear Lord,

We trust in your unfailing love and rejoice in your salvation. Apart from you, Father, I have seen we have no good thing. Please be with my children as they are at school today. Give them your help to use the words they speak to build others up, just as you command. May they begin to learn what it is like to share your love with others. You saved us so that we can share the love you have for us and in turn, love one another. Please remind us to love one another as we go about our day. I am so thankful for your love and for your work in the hearts of my children. Make your path known to them. Keep them safe as we are apart, for in you we take refuge.

In Jesus's name,
Amen

"I call on you, my God, for you will answer me; turn your ear to me and hear my prayer."

Psalm 17:6

BUS STOP PRAYERS

Dear God,

We are so blessed to come to you this morning. You, the creator of the universe, hear our prayers. As my babies leave for school this morning, I pray they take the path that leads straight to you. Keep them from the ways of those who do not want to please you. Do not let their little feet slip but hold them close to you and your teaching. I am so blessed that you hear my prayer. What comfort I take knowing I can call on you to show the wonder of your great love to my children. *You who save by your right hand, those who take refuge in you from their enemies Psalm 17:7 (NIV).* Please keep my children and future generations as the apple of your eye. Hide them in the shadow of your wings from those things that are not from you. I pray they will learn to place their focus and hope on heavenly rewards and not on the rewards of this life. We have so much to be thankful for, most of all the knowledge and love of your Son, and the hope he gives us.

In Jesus's name,
Amen

*"I love you, Lord, my strength.
The Lord is my rock, my fortress
and my deliverer; my God is
my rock, in whom I take refuge,
my shield and the horn of my
salvation, my stronghold."*

Psalm 18:1–2

*"With Your help I can advance
against a troop; with my
God I can scale a wall."*

Psalm 18:29

Dear Lord,

We love you, Father, our strength, our rock, our fortress, and deliverer. When we call to you, who is worthy of praise, we are saved from our enemies. Please teach my children how to be faithful, pure, and humble as they go through their days. Use me, family, friends, and teachers to help guide their hearts to you in all they do. When I feel weak and like I have nothing left to give, you, Lord, keep my lamp burning. You provide me with strength, patience, and love, turning my darkness into light. With your help, I can face all of the challenges in front of my family today. Your ways are perfect. Your Word is flawless. Help us place our trust in you.

In Jesus's name,
Amen

*"May these words of my mouth
and this meditation of my heart
be pleasing in your sight, Lord,
my Rock and my Redeemer."*

Psalm 19:14

BUS STOP PRAYERS

Dear God,

As we sit and wait for school to begin today, we are so humbled and thankful to be surrounded by your glory. I pray you will allow my children to see the beauty of your law, and how it revives the soul. Give us wisdom, joy in our hearts, light in our eyes. May my children learn to fear your great name. Please help them to see how your Word, when received by faith, *is more precious than gold and sweeter than honey Psalm 19:10 (NIV)*. We ask for your forgiveness of our sins. Lead us to repentance. Keep us from sin this day. When faced with choices, please guide my family to you. I pray that in all we do and say we will be pleasing in your sight, dear Father.

In Jesus's name,
Amen

*"May he give you the desire
of your heart and make all
your plans succeed."*

Psalm 20:4

BUS STOP PRAYERS

Dear God,

We trust in your name this morning, dear Lord. I pray on the days when my children are in distress and are in need of your support that you will answer their call. I pray you will give us the desires of our heart when they are according to your will. Make your desires our desires, dear Father. Help my children learn to trust in you. Raise them up to stand firm in your promises.

In Jesus's name,
Amen

*"The Lord is my shepherd,
I lack nothing."*

Psalm 23:1

Dear God,

We give you all of our thanks and glory today. Thank you for being our loving shepherd, caring for each of us. I pray my children will learn you are everything they need. Guide their paths in your righteousness. Despite being surrounded by the evil of this world, we are not afraid. You are with us, always guiding, loving, and protecting us with each step we take. Through Jesus, we have the hope of life after this world. Please let my children grow in this hope. *I pray goodness and love will follow them all the days of their lives Psalm 23:6 (NIV)*. May my family one day dwell in the house of the Lord, forever.

In Jesus's name,
Amen

"They will receive blessing from the Lord and vindication from God their Savior. Such is the generation of those who seek him, who seek your face, God of Jacob."

Psalm 24:5–6

Dear God,

As we wake this morning, we rejoice that we belong to you, dear Father. I pray you will give my children clean hands and a pure heart. I pray my children will love to seek your face. Let them receive your blessing, knowing you are the one true God. You are the king of glory, strong and mighty. We love you.
In Jesus's name,
Amen

*"In you, Lord my God,
I put my trust."*

Psalm 25:1

*"Show me your ways, Lord,
teach me your paths. Guide me
in your truth and teach me, for
you are God my Savior."*

Psalm 25:4–5

Dear God,

I lift up my children to you, God. Do not let them be put to shame or let their enemies triumph over them. Teach my children to put their hope in you. Show me your ways and teach me your Word so that I can be the mother you created me to be and lead my children to you. Guide us in your truth as we go through this day. According to your love, remember us, for you are good.

Instruct my children in your ways. Give them humble hearts so they may follow you in what is right. We rejoice in you, for all your ways are loving and faithful. Help us to keep your commands. Forgive us of our sin, so that we may remain close to you this day and listen for your instruction. I pray my children will fear your name and keep their eyes forever on you.

Guard their hearts and lives as they are apart from me this morning. Let them walk with you by their side, with integrity and uprightness, because my hope is always in you.

In Jesus's name,
Amen

*"One thing I ask from the Lord,
this only do I seek: that I may
dwell in the house of the Lord
all the days of my life, to gaze
on the beauty of the Lord and
to seek him in his temple."*

Psalm 27:4

BUS STOP PRAYERS

Dear God,

You alone are our light and salvation—whom shall we fear? You are the stronghold of our lives—of whom shall we be afraid? I pray you keep my children safe from the enemies in this world. When they try to attack my precious children they will stumble and fall.

Father, continue to guide my children to your truth. I will remain confident and without fear that you are with my children each day, pointing them to you. You know my heart, dear Lord, that I ask you one thing:

I pray that my children and husband will dwell in the house of the Lord all the days of their lives, and gaze upon the beauty of the Lord, and seek him in his temple. Hide my children in the shelter of your tabernacle, set them high upon a rock. Help my family to shout with joy, to sing and make music to the Lord. As a mother of small children, *hear my voice when I call, o Lord, be merciful to me and answer me, my heart says of you, "seek his face!" Your face, Lord, I will seek Psalm 27:7-8 (NIV)* so that I may lead my children to you. Help me for I cannot do this alone. Teach my children your way, o Lord, lead them in a straight path, do not let them turn to the desires of their own hearts, or allow lies to mislead them.

I am confident in my prayer to you, o Lord, that you will answer and that you are working in the hearts of my babies even though I can't always see it. I am confident I will see the goodness of the Lord come to fruition in my children, but in the meantime I wait for the Lord, and your perfect timing. Help me to be strong and take heart while I wait on the Lord.

In Jesus's name,

Amen

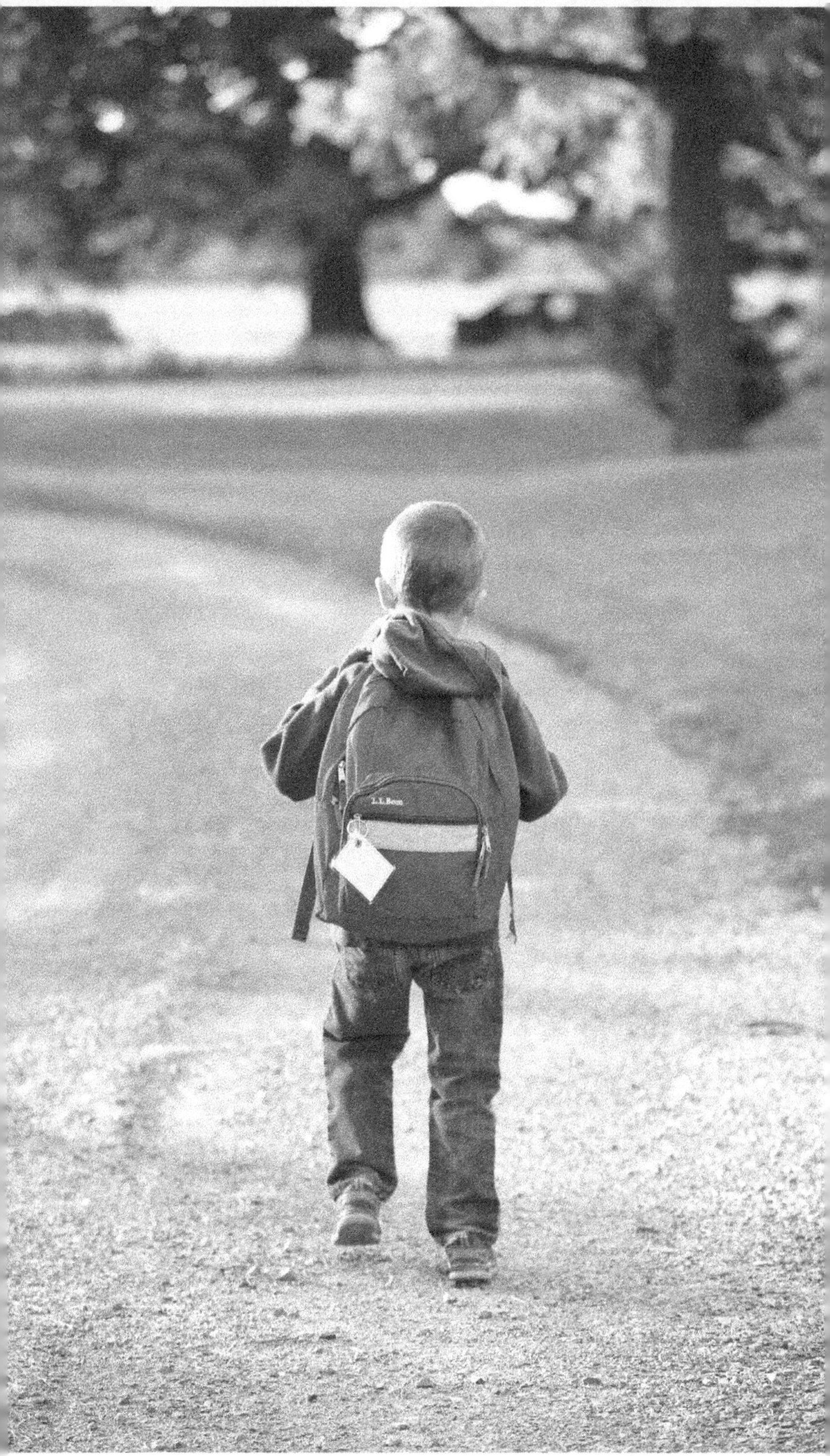

"The Lord is my strength and my shield; my heart trusts in him, and he helps me."

Psalm 28:7

"Save your people and bless your inheritance; be their shepherd and carry them forever."

Psalm 28:9

Dear Lord,

To you I call, o Lord, my rock, on this morning. Please hear our cry for your help as we lift our hands to you and go through our day. Do not let my children be led astray by this world, but keep their hearts close to you. We praise your name, for you hear our cries for mercy. Let us remember you are our strength and shield. Teach my children to let their hearts trust in you, that you are their great helper. *My heart leaps for joy knowing you are the strength of your people, a fortress of salvation for his anointed one Psalm 28:7-8 (NIV).* Save my children. Be their shepherd and carry them forever.

In Jesus's name,
Amen

*"Ascribe to the Lord the glory
due his name; worship the Lord
in the splendor of his holiness."*

Psalm 29:2

*"…the Lord is enthroned
as King forever."*

Psalm 29:10

Dear God,

Thank you for always meeting us, every morning before school. Teach my children to know and feel the "awe" that is your name, the Lord of all creation, our holy king. Your voice is everywhere, powerful and majestic, nothing is impossible for you. Please give us strength for today, and bless us with your peace.
In Jesus's name,
Amen

*"You turned my wailing into
dancing; you removed my sackcloth
and clothed me with joy, that my
heart may sing your praises and
not be silent. Lord, my God,
I will praise you forever."*

Psalm 30:11–12

Dear God,

We praise your name this morning, o Lord, for your mercy and grace has given us this day. Please help my children to understand although tough times can come living as God's child, difficulties don't last forever. Your care does. *We may weep for a night, but joy comes in the morning Psalm 30:5 (NIV)*. Teach them to seek you when they need help. Bring them peace that you can turn darkness into light. Let their hearts sing to you and not be silent, always ready to give thanks.

In Jesus's name,
Amen

"Since you are my rock and my fortress, for the sake of your name lead and guide me…"

Psalm 31:3

"Let your face shine on your servant; save me in your unfailing love."

Psalm 31:16

BUS STOP PRAYERS

Dear God,

Thank you God for all the times you bring us back to you and to your Word. Grant us focus to continue in fellowship and love with you, so we may do your work. My children are yours, I lift them up to you in prayer. Please deliver my children in your righteousness, never let them be put to shame. I pray they know you are their rock and refuge, a strong fortress that will save them. *For the sake of your name, lead and guide my children in your will Psalm 31:3 (NIV)*. Free them from the traps set for them. Into your hands I commit my children, redeem them, o Lord, the God of Truth. I pray my children will not cling to worthless idols, but place their trust in you. Help us to rejoice in your love and not grow weak by focusing on the enemy around us. Instead, help us to keep our focus on you. Let my children proclaim, "You are my God." Their times are in your hands, let your face shine on them, save them in your unfailing love. *How great is your goodness, which you have stored up for those who fear you Psalm 31:19 (NIV)*. Praise be to your name! Allow my children to become faithful and not proud, to be strong and take heart, hoping in the Lord.

In Jesus's name,
Amen

"Then I acknowledged my sin to you and did not cover up my iniquity. I said, 'I will confess my transgressions to the Lord. And you forgave the guilt of my sin.'"

Psalm 32:5

"I will instruct you and teach you in the way you should go; I will counsel you with my loving eye on you."

Psalm 32:8

Dear God,

We are so blessed to know you are here for us, our rock and refuge. You are here for us to confess our sins. You promise to make us righteous through your Son. I pray my children will learn to come to you right away when they have sinned and ask for your forgiveness so they will stand blameless in your sight. I pray they will understand only you can remove the guilt our sin brings. Help me instruct my children and teach them the way they should go. Watch over them as they are away at school today and each day as they grow. I pray for your unfailing love to surround them as they learn to place their trust in you. Because you have forgiven our sin, we can stand upright and sing your praises, rejoicing in your name.

In Jesus's name,
Amen

*"For the word of the Lord
is right and true; He is
faithful in all he does."*

Psalm 33:4

*"But the plans of the Lord stand
firm forever, the purposes of his
heart through all generations."*

Psalm 33:11

BUS STOP PRAYERS

Dear God,

We lift joyful voices in praise to you, this morning, dear Father, for your word is right and true. You are faithful in all you do. I pray my children will learn to love righteousness and justice, just like you. Speak to their hearts and let them know they are surrounded by your unfailing love on the days when they fail.

I pray they recognize the wonder in all of your creation, learn to fear your name, and hear your voice. Allow them to not rely on their own plans, but to know your plans stand firm forever, along with your purpose.

I pray my children will make you their Lord, placing their hope in you. Keep your eyes upon their lives. May they experience you as their hope and shield, only to rejoice in your holy name.

May your unfailing love rest upon us, o Lord, as we put our hope in you.

In Jesus's name,
Amen

"Glorify the Lord with me; let us exalt his name together. I sought the Lord, and he answered me; he delivered me from all my fears. Those who look to him are radiant; their faces are never covered with shame."

Psalm 34:3–5

"Come, my children, listen to me; I will teach you the fear of the Lord."

Psalm 34:11

Dear God,

I lift my children up to you this morning, o Lord, praying for your praise to be on their lips at all times. Please let them bring glory to you in all they do, always ready and willing to give you the credit for everything good in their lives. Let us exalt your name together as a family. I pray my children will want to seek you with their whole heart, and as you promise, you will answer and deliver them from all their fears. Make their faces radiant, so that when others see them they see your love. Please keep them from bringing shame to themselves or to you. Help me to teach my children to fear your name, so that they will see many good days. I pray you will watch over their words, keeping their tongues from evil, and their lips from speaking lies. As they grow, help them to turn from evil and do good, and to seek peace and pursue it. When they are in trouble, I pray they learn to turn to you to deliver and protect them. Let my children take refuge in you, so they will not be condemned, but stand in your glory and righteousness.

In Jesus's name,
Amen

*"Do not be far from me,
Lord. Awake, and rise to
my defense! Contend for me,
my God and Lord."*

Psalm 35:22–23

BUS STOP PRAYERS

Dear God,

I am seeing how much my children and I are up against as they spend more time away from home. I have to admit sometimes I feel afraid and defeated. Then I remember, you have already defeated the world through Jesus and for that reason I lay this concern at your feet. Fight against those who fight against my children. I have faith that through you it is possible to raise children who are pure, moral, just, loving, and filled with the Holy Spirit. Please keep my eyes and thoughts on you and not in other directions. Let me not feel defeated, o Lord, but strengthened, equipped by you to be the mother you made me to be: filled with courage, wisdom, energy, and joy. May your angels drive away the enemy from my children. Help me to equip them through you, so they can recognize what is good and what is not from you. Help us to stay close and connected to you, in constant communication. I pray this so we can do your will and bring glory to your name. Do not allow this world to swallow up my children. They are set apart for you and your works. For we will speak of your righteousness and of your praises all day long.
    In Jesus's name,
    Amen

*"How priceless is your
unfailing love, o God!"*

Psalm 36:7

*"For with you is the fountain of
life; in your light we see light."*

Psalm 36:9

BUS STOP PRAYERS

Dear Father,

We are so thankful for your love. *Your love reaches to the heavens, your faithfulness to the skies. Your righteousness is like the mighty mountains, your justice like the great deep. How priceless is your unfailing love Psalm 36:6 (NIV)*. Please teach my children the goodness of your love and to how to find refuge in the shadow of your wings. I pray they will *feast on the abundance of your house, drink from the river of your delights Psalm 36:8 (NIV)*. You alone give life, and through your Son, eternal life. Let your light shine on the faces of my children, so through them others will see you.

I pray you *continue your love to those who know you, your righteousness to the upright in heart Psalm 36:10 (NIV)*. May my children never become proud or influenced by others who are proud. Keep the hands of the wicked away from my children as they grow. Allow their only influence to be by your Spirit and others who know your love. Please bring godly influences into their lives as they continue to grow in the knowledge and love of Christ.

In Jesus's name,
Amen

"I was young and now I am old, yet I have never seen the righteous forsaken or their children begging bread. They are always generous and lend freely; their children will be a blessing."

Psalm 37:25–26

BUS STOP PRAYERS

Dear God,

Thank you Father for your continued work in the hearts of my children. You know my inner most thoughts and feelings and I give them all to you. Replace my fears and worries with peace, patience, wisdom, and understanding. My prayer for my children is that you will help me teach them to trust in you and do your good. May they delight in you so that your desires will become their desires. I pray they will commit their ways to you. Make them righteous radiant in your light.

In this world we live in, it can be such a challenge for us to quiet our souls. Allow my children to learn how to be still before the Lord and to wait patiently for you. I know this skill will make a profound impact on their lives and their ability to do your work. Help me to keep this command myself and teach it to my children.

Help them to refrain from anger and turn from wrath, but instead to keep their hope in you. Fill my children with a meek spirit, so they can inherit your kingdom and enjoy great peace. I pray for their hearts that they will give generously at all times and turn from selfishness. Make their steps firm. Let them know even when they stumble they will not fall because you are there to uphold them with your hand. Let them know you will always provide for all of their needs, to depend on you alone for everything.

Make my children turn from evil and do good, so they will dwell in the land forever. *You love the just and will not forsake your faithful ones Psalm 37:28 (NIV)*. Thank you, Father, that you will protect my children forever. Watch over their tongues that they learn to only speak with wisdom. I pray your law is forever in their hearts, and their feet will not slip.

In Jesus's name,
Amen

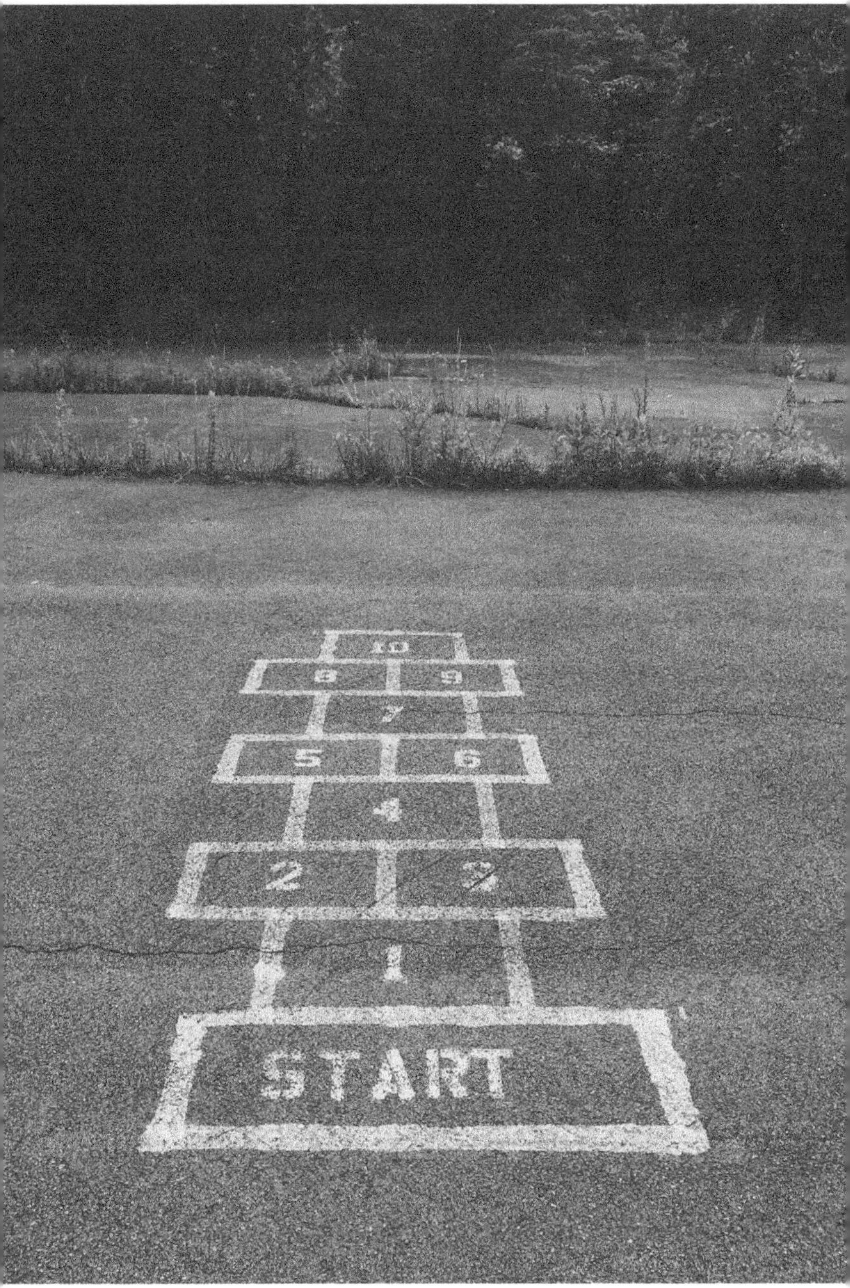
10
8
9
7
5
6
4
2
3
1
START

"I waited patiently for the Lord; he turned to me and heard my cry."

Psalm 40:1

"I desire to do your will, my God; your law is within my heart."

Psalm 40:8

Dear God,

My heart is filled with joy and thanks today. I praise your name for you are so good. You hear my prayer and know my heart even when I don't know what to say. You lift me out of my self-pity, and raise me up, giving me a new song and new motivation to be the mother and person you created me to be. I feel secure because of your promises and care for me. I know being home with my children is a call from you. I am right where I need to be. Thank you for renewing my faith, my spirit, my energy for you and for teaching my children. I praise your name for all your ways are good.

So many times you have answered my longing for more, by helping me to feel content. You set my feet upon a rock and gave me a firm place to stand. I pray my children will be blessed by this renewal, and will see, fear, and put their trust in the Lord. Let them not turn to the proud or put their trust in false gods. Help them to learn of the many wonders you have done and know that you are good.

Fill us with the desire to do your will by hiding your Word in our hearts. *Let us make known your righteousness and never hide your love, truth, faithfulness, or salvation. Do not withhold your mercy from us, o Lord, may your love and your truth always protect me Psalm 40:10-11 (NIV)*. For I see more and more each day the troubles and sins around us. *My heart fails within me Psalm 40:12 (NIV)*. Be pleased, o Lord, to save me, my husband, and my children, come quickly to help us. Keep all harm and evil away from our family. *May all who seek you rejoice and be glad in you, may those who love your salvation always say, "The Lord be exalted!" Psalm 40:16 (NIV)*. We need you, dear Father, may you think of us, you are our help and our deliverer, o my God, do not delay *Psalm 40:17 (NIV)*.

In Jesus's name,
Amen

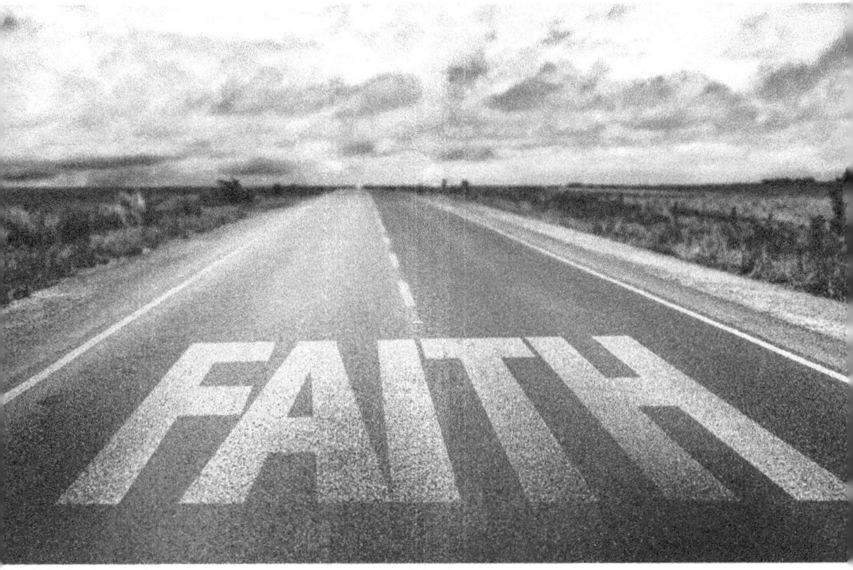
FAITH

"...Have mercy on me, Lord; heal me, for I have sinned against you."

Psalm 41:4

Dear God,

I pray that you will give my children a heart for the weak. I pray they will know of your great love and the mercy you show us every day. In turn, let them show mercy to others. Please protect and sustain our children this day, Father. Let them see it is you who provides for all of their needs. Help my husband and I to be a godly example, cleanse us of our own sinful ways, and let us walk in the path you have set for our family. It is so good to see you at work in our hearts and in our family. Let their hearts be soft and willing to accept your Word. Ultimately, I look forward to the day when my children truly understand their need for a savior, your Son, Jesus Christ. Thank you for never giving up on me, or on us, that alone brings me such comfort and hope for the future.

You are everything to me. I lift your name on high and rejoice that you are my heavenly Father.

In Jesus's name,
Amen

*"By day the Lord directs his love,
at night his song is with me—a
prayer to the God of my life."*

Psalm 42:8

Dear God,

You never let go, dear Father, and for that I am thankful. When I seek you, you are there to renew my hope. I pray I will seek you more each day. Teach my children to place their hope in you alone. Allow their souls to thirst for you, to yearn for your Word. We praise your name, our Savior, our God. I take comfort in knowing your love is directed by day and at night your song is with us. Each day we are surrounded by the despair and evil in this world, but we have placed our hope in you. Let us be filled with peace and free from fear.

I also pray that one day when someone asks my children, "Where is your God?" they will be able to answer according to your glorious will and with great faith. May your love and grace pour out through them.

I love you, my Father.
In Jesus's name,
Amen

*"Send me your light and your
faithful care, let them lead me;"*

Psalm 43:3

Dear God,

You are our God, our stronghold. Set forth your light and your truth as a guide for my children. Even when things don't go their way, let their hearts make you their joy and delight as they learn to place their hope in you.

Praise be to your name, our Savior, our God.

In Jesus's name,
Amen

"It was not by their sword that they won the land, nor did their arm bring them victory; it was your right hand, your arm, and the light of your face, for you loved them."

Psalm 44:3

Dear God,

Please let my children love to hear of your glorious works long ago. Help them to witness your continued work today. Do not let them become proud of their God-given talents, but that in everything they will give you the glory. I pray they are infused with the courage to speak your name no matter where they are. For everything we have, we do, and we are, should be for your glory. May my children and their future generations know it is you at work, not because of their own hands. Rescue and redeem my children and their future generations because of your unfailing love.

In Jesus's name,
Amen

"You love righteousness and hate wickedness; therefore God, your God, has set you above your companions by anointing you with the oil of joy."

Psalm 45:7

Dear God,

Teach my children to love righteousness and despise wickedness. Anoint them with the oil of joy. My most heartfelt prayer is that the generations of children I leave behind will perpetuate your memory through each new child. May my legacy be to have brought glory to you by leaving behind generations of men and women after your own heart, who will praise you forever.
In Jesus's name,
Amen

"He says, 'Be still, and know that I am God; I will be exalted among the nations, I will be exalted in the earth.'"

Psalm 46:10

BUS STOP PRAYERS

Dear God,

You remain my refuge and strength, always there to help me in times of trouble. Sometimes I feel as though the troubles of this world and danger that surrounds my family can be overwhelming, until I remember you are with us. Forgive me for when I keep trying to do things on my own and forget to communicate with you throughout every moment, big and small, during my day. I pray my children will always look to you to be their strength and find refuge in your Word and love. Help me to teach my children to be still and know that you are God. What an amazing verse and one that I find I struggle with living in our fast-paced world. Allow us to take advantage of opportunities you give us where we can be still and reflect on you. Give us times of peace and quiet and let us use those times to be with you. I pray you will speak to my children, for they have told me they want to learn to hear your voice. Teach their hearts to know you and their minds to be focused on you. Anything is possible with you. I know I can depend on you to do great things within the children you gave me, things that I cannot do on my own.

I love you.
In Jesus's name,
Amen

"Sing praises to God, sing praises; sing praises to our King, sing praises."

Psalm 47:6

Dear God,

We wake to you this morning with joy in our hearts, for you are the King over all the earth! No matter what today brings, we can be sure you know what is best for us. Please guide the footsteps of my children to walk in your will. Help my children to know that joy is not dependent upon what is happening to us, but that it comes from knowing your great love for all people through your Son, Jesus.

We praise your name, for who you are, not just for what you have done.

In Jesus's name,
Amen

*"...We meditate on Your
unfailing love."*

Psalm 48:9

Dear God,

You are so good to us, dear Father, even though we don't deserve all that you have given us. My prayer today is that you will teach my children how to be good to others and love like you do, even though the other person may not be deserving of it. Help us love those who are hard to love, so that you will be made known through the actions of our family.
In Jesus's name,
Amen

"People who have wealth but lack understanding are like the beasts that perish."

Psalm 49:20

Dear God,

I pray this morning for the hearts of my children. May you teach them about what is most important in life. Let them not become distracted or blinded by wealth, success, or acquiring more "things," but instead they will be humble, hardworking, and put you above all else. I pray they will gain wisdom from a young age and everything that flows from their heart will be for good. Please allow them to have awareness for the life you promise after our time on earth. Let them see that this world is not all we have. Instead, through your Son, Jesus, we have the most amazing hope to hold on to, no matter what is happening around us.

In Jesus's name,
Amen

"And call on me in the day of trouble; I will deliver you, and you will honor me."

Psalm 50:15

Dear God,

Thank you for this morning and for your perfect will. You make the sun rise and set each day, giving us a new opportunity to love and forgive like you do. My prayer for my children this morning is that they will fear your holy name, and grow in their understanding of not only your great works, but of who you are as well. I pray they will be covered with the grace of Jesus when it is time for your judgment. May this grace you freely give to us be extended to others through my family. Please let my children know they cannot manipulate your plans or bargain with you. Teach them that what really matters is the attitude they bring to you and how you alone are enough.

In Jesus's name,
Amen

*"Have mercy on me, o God,
according to your unfailing love;
according to your great compassion
blot out my transgressions.
Wash away all my iniquity and
cleanse me from my sin."*

Psalm 51:1–2

Dear God,

We come to you asking for forgiveness of our sins and pray your scripture:

> *Create in me a pure heart, o God, and renew a steadfast spirit within me. Do not cast me from your presence or take Your Holy Spirit from me. Restore to me the joy of your salvation and grant me a willing spirit, to sustain me Psalm 51:10–13 (NIV).*

Help me to be eager to make time for you each day, so my children and my home will be blessed by your holy presence. I pray that we will not take for granted the incredible gift you have given us, in your Son, Jesus, and all of the many wonderful blessings you have given our family. Allow my children to never make themselves more important than you and doing your kingdom work. I pray they will know how small they are in this great universe and be humbled by your creation. The world seems to grow more and more obsessed with "self." I pray you keep the hearts of my children far from the world in that regard, so they will always look to put you and the needs of others above their own selfish desires. Give them the strength to stand up to kids at school who may look down on them for being "different." When this does happen, let their words be filled with love and grace.

I am so thankful to have you, Father, by my side as my children are growing and going into the world. Be by their side, every moment of every day, speaking, guiding, loving, and protecting, as only you can do.

In Jesus's name,
Amen

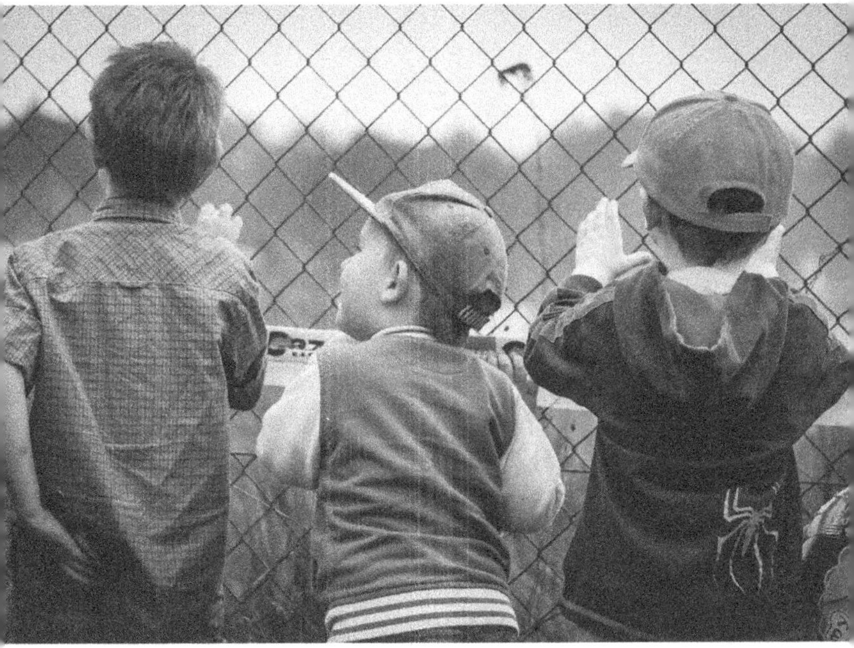

*"I trust in God's unfailing
love for ever and ever."*

Psalm 52:8

*"And I will hope in your name,
for your name is good."*

Psalm 52:9

Thank you Father for giving us joy each day and I pray my children will carry on that joy throughout their lives. Although evil surrounds us, I know we are safe when we stay close to you. I pray my children will be lovers of good and truth, not of evil and falsehood. Help us teach them how to stay close to you, to grow in a relationship with their heavenly Father. Never let them place you in a "Sunday only" spot in their lives. Let us show our children how to make you a part of our everyday lives, to communicate with you all day and all night, knowing you want to be a part of everything—big and small, easy and difficult, good and bad. Thank you, Father, for hearing my prayer. You are my everything.

In Jesus's name,
Amen

"God looks down from heaven on all mankind to see if there are any who understand, any who seek God."

Psalm 53:2

Dear God,

I pray my children will begin to learn what it means to seek you, Father, with all their heart, so they will find you, as you have promised. Help my children begin to hear your voice and know your will from an early age. I pray they will always know your love in their heart and be willing to speak of that love to others. May you be shaping and growing my children every day into the people you created them to be. When I am blessed enough to witness those moments when you are at work in my children, my heart is filled with such amazement and gratitude. I am continually thankful for your grace and for the strength you give me each day. Let me as their mother never grow weary in doing good and to continue on toward the goal you have given me.

In Jesus's name,
Amen

"Hear my prayer, o God; listen to the words of my mouth."

Psalm 54:2

"Surely God is my help; the Lord is the one who sustains me."

Psalm 54:4

BUS STOP PRAYERS

Dear God,

Save my children, o God, by your name, vindicate them by your might Psalm 54:1 (NIV). How grateful I am that you hear all of my prayers. The world and its evil surround us, but I will not lose hope. I believe with all my heart you are my help. How grateful I am for your sustenance. Help me to trust in you as my children grow, for they do not belong to me, but to you. I will praise your name, o Lord, for it is good.

In Jesus's name,
Amen

"As for me, I call to God, and the Lord saves me. Evening, morning and noon I cry out in distress, and he hears my voice. He rescues me unharmed from the battle waged against me, even though many oppose me."

Psalm 55:16–18

Dear God,

Each day we wake we are so thankful for your love and grace. Thank you, Father, for hearing my prayers, my cries for help, and my words of praise. I know in my heart you are here to rescue us from this fallen world because of your Son, Jesus, and his work on the cross.

Help us to remain thankful today for all things at all times. I pray we remember to give our worries to you in complete trust. Your word says, *He will sustain you; he will never let the righteous be shaken Psalm 55:22 (NIV)*. I pray my children will learn what it means to truly trust you at an early age and depend on you for all their needs, knowing you are their heavenly Father who has amazing plans for them.

In Jesus's name,
Amen

"In God, whose word I praise, in the Lord, whose word I praise—in God I trust and am not afraid. What can man do to me?"

Psalm 56:10-11

Dear God,

It is my deepest heartfelt prayer that my children will learn to grow up with a true, loving relationship with you. Hear our prayer that when my children are afraid, they will *trust in you, in God, whose word I praise Psalm 56:4 (NIV)*. May they not be afraid and know that man can do nothing to their soul and the salvation you give them through your Son, Jesus Christ.

I present my thank offering to you, for you have delivered me from death, and my feet from stumbling that I may walk before you in the light of life Psalm 56:12-13 (NIV). I pray for you, my Father, to deliver my children and keep their paths straight. May they also walk before you in the light of life.

In Jesus's name,
Amen

*"God sends forth his love
and his faithfulness."*

Psalm 57:3

BUS STOP PRAYERS

Dear God,

How thankful I am as a mother, surrounded by the world around me, that you promise to send your love and faithfulness. Give me a heart that is dedicated to you and the kingdom work you have given me in raising my children. I pray for the hearts of my children that they will become girls and boys, and then women and men after your own heart. Even at such a young age, give them a steadfast heart, *awaken their souls to your Word, your grace, your purpose for them.*

I praise you, Father, for who you are. Let my children see how great is your love, reaching to the heavens, your faithfulness reaching to the skies. *Be exalted, o God, above the heavens, let your glory be over all the earth Psalm 57:11 (NIV).*

In Jesus's name,
Amen

"Deliver me from my enemies, o God; be my fortress against those who are attacking me."

Psalm 59:1

"Save us and help us with your right hand, that those you love may be delivered."

Psalm 60:5

BUS STOP PRAYERS

Dear God,

Help us to remember to sing of your strength and love before we rise each morning, to offer our praises to you and allow you to be in our hearts as we begin a new day. I pray as my children go about their day, they will remember you are their fortress and refuge in times of trouble, for you are their loving God. Save my children with your right hand that they will not choose their own way but the way you have set for them.

Forgive me, Father, for when my mind is weak and I let in doubt from the enemy. You alone have the power to save my family and bring them to salvation. I believe with all my heart that your promises are true. The life you seek for my children is not impossible and forgive me when I think it is. I am sorry when I look around at the world and feel defeated. You have already defeated the world. Answer my prayers, Father, and make my children who you created them to be.

In Jesus's name,
Amen

"Trust in him at all times, you people; pour out your hearts to him, for God is our refuge."

Psalm 62:8

Dear God,

I pray with all the distractions, opportunities, and daily tasks to do in this world that my children will learn to find rest in you alone. I pray they will learn to seek your Word and stay in your presence. Each day I wake with the sole purpose of guiding my children to you, dear Father, knowing that their salvation can only come from you. Keep me focused in this responsibility. Let my children see you as their fortress and hope so they will not be shaken by life's problems.

I see how you have put "dependence" on my heart and I pray you will help me show my children how beautiful dependence upon you really is. Thank you for teaching me that our prayers are glorious to you because they show our humble dependence upon you, our Creator. Teach my children to trust in you at all times and how to pour their hearts out to you, for you, God, are our refuge.

In Jesus's name,
Amen

"You, God, are my God, earnestly I seek you; I thirst for you, my whole being longs for you, in a dry and parched land where there is no water."

Psalm 63:1

Dear Father,

You know my heart and that I want nothing more than for my children to call you Father and to love your Son. I want to see my children become exactly who you made them to be, fulfilling your purpose in the work you give them each day. I know the years I have now where they are home with me are short and I pray you help me to make the most of each day, that your Word and lessons of wisdom, love, and service are tucked deep in the hearts and minds of my children. I pray they earnestly seek your face from a young age and know that nothing this world can offer will bring them the satisfaction only you can give. Let my children remember to talk with you during those quiet moments as they fall asleep and think of you through the night. Keep my children humble and grateful that they will know it is because of you they are blessed with whatever gifts and talents you have chosen to give them. I pray they sing your praises from the shadow of your wings, knowing you are their help for all they do. Never let my children stray from your right hand. I thank you for all the work you are doing in the hearts of my children that I see and for the work I cannot see.

In Jesus's name,
Amen

"All people will fear; they will proclaim the works of God and ponder what he has done."

Psalm 64:9

Dear God,

Thank you Father for giving me the gift of motherhood and for teaching me to trust in you. One of the greatest lessons you taught me is that my children *belong to you, not to me*. It can be so hard at times to let go and to fully trust. Forgive me when I am weak. You know I constantly pray for protection over my precious children and I am thankful you hear my prayers. You give me comfort, knowing you are at work. I continue to pray for you to keep the evil of this world away from my children. Instead of being led astray, let them be led to you. Help me teach my children to test everything against your Word, so they may know and follow the truth. I pray my children will fear your name, proclaim your works, rejoice in you, and become upright of heart because of your Son.

In Jesus's name,
Amen

"You answer us with awesome and righteous deeds, God our Savior, the hope of all the ends of the earth…"

Psalm 65:5

BUS STOP PRAYERS

Dear God,

There are so many times during these days of motherhood where I feel overwhelmed by everything—including my own faults. Your Word says you are faithful and hear my prayers. Help me to let go of my anxieties, fears, and problems. I bring these to you and lay them at your feet. Forgive me for not always seeing the opportunities you give me to trust you.

Thank you, Father, for bringing us close to you and giving us so many blessings we do not deserve. Please continue to bring my children and my husband close to you, so they will be filled with the good things of your house, your holy temple. I am so thankful you answer my prayers with awesome deeds of righteousness, for you are my Savior, my hope, my strength. Just as you care for your beautiful creation, you take care of me and my family, and I am so grateful. We owe everything we have to you. I pray you will give me, my husband, and my children wisdom to use these blessings for your glory. When I began writing this prayer along with your Word, I was feeling low, and I am amazed by your work once again. Just by reading your Psalm my spirit has been lifted and filled with such joy and hope. I praise your name and pray my children will learn to experience a full and loving relationship with you.

In Jesus's name,
Amen

*"Praise our God, all peoples, let
the sound of his praise be heard;
he has preserved our lives and
kept our feet from slipping."*

Psalm 66:8–9

Dear God,

This morning as we greet you, dear Father, our hearts shout for joy and sing of the glory of your name. I love you, Father, for who you are, not just for what you do. I pray that my children will be so moved by your scripture that they will proclaim, *How awesome are your deeds! Psalm 66:3 (NIV)*. I pray they will want to sing praises to you and to share your love with others. You are at work now, refining my children like silver, as they grow. I pray when the time comes, all of my children will be able to say to those who listen, *Let me tell you what he has done for me Psalm 66:16 (NIV)*. When they are going through hard times, I pray praise will be upon their lips. Let our family not cherish sin in our heart, but instead let us confess our sins to you so you will listen and hear our voices in prayer. I praise you, God, for you hear all of my prayers. Despite all that is wrong with me, you never withhold your love from me and I am so grateful.

In Jesus's name,
Amen

"May God be gracious to us and bless us and make his face shine on us—so that your way may be known on earth, your salvation among all nations."

Psalm 67:1–2

Dear God,

May you be gracious and bless my children this morning, o God. Make your *face shine upon them, so that others will know your ways and your salvation*. Let my children praise your name, be glad and sing for joy, because you are in control. Every day guide my children in your ways, speak to them, and let your voice be known. My children ask me how they can hear your voice. Please make your voice known to them.

My prayer is that after all these years of child rearing, the children you gave me will produce a great harvest in your name, and that all will know it is because of you alone.

In Jesus's name,
Amen

"Praise be to the Lord, to God our Savior, who daily bears our burdens. Our God is a God who saves; from the Sovereign Lord comes escape from death."

Psalm 68:19–20

Dear God,

I pray to you this morning for the protection of my children from this world. Make their hearts rejoice before you. Let them be filled with happiness and joy.

You are everything to us, our Father. I have come to realize how much we need to recognize our dependence upon you and how beautiful that is. Continue to show our family how to depend on you each day, to rely on your power and strength, and to communicate with you through everything going on in our lives. Your knowledge and way is perfect. You understand all. I am growing in trust knowing this.

Praise be to God!
In Jesus's name,
Amen

"But I pray to you, Lord, in the time of your favor; in your great love, o God, answer me with your sure salvation."

Psalm 69:13

Dear God,

Save me, o God, for there are many times lately when I let myself feel overwhelmed, defeated and tired. In these moments, help me to direct my thoughts to you and remember my purpose while leaning upon your word for strength and encouragement. Rescue me from my thoughts when they are not pleasing to you, so that I may be an example of your love to my family. I pray for my children to understand this as they grow, to call on you when they feel weak or when their thoughts are not in line with your word. I am so thankful for your love and that you are faithful.

In Jesus's name,
Amen

"But as for me, I am poor and needy; come quickly to me, o God. You are my help and my deliverer; Lord, do not delay."

Psalm 70:5

Dear God,

I call upon your name for help this morning. Keep the enemy away from my family. Teach us to know when we are being attacked by things that are not from you. Give us your strength, wisdom, perseverance, and thanksgiving to make it through. We rejoice and are glad in you, alone, God, and praise your name each day. I am realizing more and more my dependence upon you and pray that my children will recognize their weakness and turn to you for strength.

In Jesus's name,
Amen

"Since my youth, God, you have taught me, and to this day I declare your marvelous deeds. Even when I am old and gray, do not forsake me, my God, till I declare your power to the next generation, your mighty acts to all who are to come."

Psalm 71:17-18

Dear God,

I pray my children will take refuge in you, let them never be put to shame. Rescue and deliver my family in your righteousness, turn your ear to them and save them. When they are in need, let them turn to you first before all others. Deliver my family, o my God, from the hand of the wicked, from the grasp of evil. Let my children see you as their hope, that they will be confident in your promises from a young age. Allow their little hearts to gain deep wisdom and trust in your word, for this is my greatest desire since I first found out you were going to bless me with the gift of motherhood. May the lips of my children praise your name and declare your splendor all day long.

Be not far from my children, o God, come quickly to help them Psalm 71:12 (NIV). Give me and my entire family strength and perseverance to live for you, despite what others may think or say. When we encounter negativity, instead of falling into despair or giving up our hope, let us grow stronger in faith, and tell of your righteousness and salvation all day long. As my children are young, I pray they learn your word and of your mighty deeds, and will speak of them to others and to their children, who will continue to pass down the truth of your love and salvation.

Your righteousness reaches to the heavens, you who have done great things. Who is like you, God? Psalm 71:19 (NIV). Let my children understand that they will see troubles, but those troubles will not last. Instead, I pray my children will place their hope in the one day you will restore our lives forever.

I pray I will see my children rejoice and sing your praises for the redemption you offer them. While I wait in hope for this day, I pray for your strength, courage, creativity, wisdom, and perseverance to continue teaching your love and building our home on the foundation of your word.

In Jesus's name,
Amen

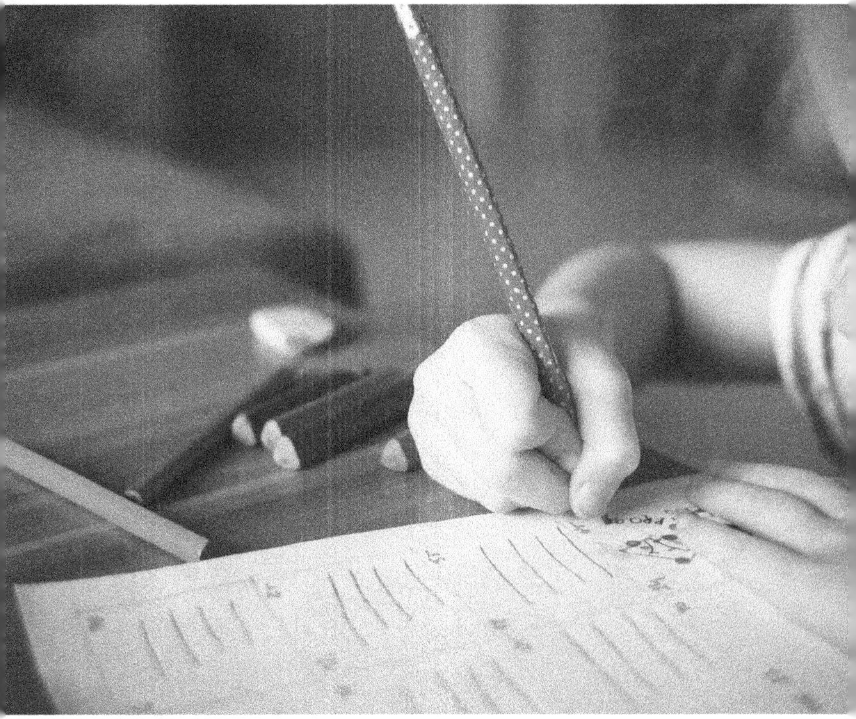

*"My flesh and my heart may fail,
but God is the strength of my
heart and my portion forever."*

Psalm 73:26

Dear God,

I pray you will give my children an eternal perspective, dear Father. Let their hearts be pure and focused on serving you and doing your will. Do not allow anything from this world gain a stronghold in their hearts or minds. Instead, I pray they learn to store up treasures in heaven, knowing the only things truly worthwhile are those that are eternal. Keep envy, greed, and jealousy away from them. If it does begin to creep in, I pray they will be quickly brought to repentance.

Guide my children with your counsel, let earth have nothing they desire but you Psalm 73:24–25 (NIV).

In Jesus's name,
Amen

*"But God is my king from long ago;
he brings salvation on the earth."*

Psalm 74:12

Dear God,

It is my prayer to you, dear Father, that my children will learn to fear your great name. I pray they will truly try to grasp the power and glory of your works. When they see your greatness, they will also see how you have chosen to place your mercy upon us. It was your choice not to condemn us but to give us eternal life. We give thanks and praise your name, for you, Father, are good.
In Jesus's name,
Amen

"We praise you, God, we praise you, for your name is near; people tell of your wonderful deeds."

Psalm 75:1

Dear God,

I pray my children will hear of your wonderful deeds and store your works in their heart. Help my children to give themselves to you and have faith in Jesus, so when your time of judgment comes, they will be clothed in his righteousness. Let them not become boastful or proud, but in everything, let them learn to acknowledge you as the source for all that they are. I pray they will sing your praises all the days of their lives.

In Jesus's name,
Amen

"Your ways, God, are holy. What god is as great as our God? You are the God who performs miracles; you display your power among the peoples. With your mighty arm you redeemed your people."

Psalm 77:13–15

Dear God,

Thank you, dear Father, for you alone are good. When my children begin to feel afraid, anxious, worried, or like you are not there, let them be reminded of all the ways you carried them in the past. May they remember all of the good works you were secretly working on behind the scenes, and how you came through on your promises, which stand firm forever. Let them trust that your plans are always for the good of those who love you, to give them hope and a future. Your ways are holy and not like our ways. You are the God who performs miracles. Have my children grow to place their trust in you alone, in good times and in bad.

In Jesus's name,
Amen

"We will tell the next generation the praiseworthy deeds of the Lord, his power, and the wonders he has done. He decreed statutes for Jacob and established the law in Israel, which he commanded our ancestors to teach their children, so the next generation would know them, even the children yet to be born, and they in turn would tell their children. Then they would put their trust in God and would not forget his deeds but would keep his commands."

Psalm 78:4–7

BUS STOP PRAYERS

Dear God,

I pray for you to give my children listening ears and an open heart. Give my husband and me the ability to teach your Word to our children in our home, so that we can tell them the praiseworthy deeds of the Lord, his power, and the wonders he has done. I pray you grow a passion for your Word in their hearts, one that will never end as long as they live. May they tell their children the wonders of your great love and they in turn will tell their children and all the generations to come. Then they would put their trust in God and would not forget his deeds but would keep his commands. Do not let my children or their children become stubborn and rebellious, it would pain my heart beyond words to see them not follow you. Instead make their hearts loyal and faithful to you. Help my children to remember the wonders you have done. I pray what they are learning as children will carry with them throughout their entire lives. I pray they learn to look at your faithfulness in the past and use that faithfulness to trust you with the future. In good times, not just in bad, I pray my children will seek your face continually. I pray they will want to draw near to you in prayer because of their sincere belief in you, our Father, and your Son.

In Jesus's name,
Amen

"Do not hold against us the sins of past generations; may your mercy come quickly to meet us, for we are in desperate need. Help us, God, our Savior, for the glory of your name; deliver us and forgive our sins for your name's sake."

Psalm 79:8–9

Dear God,

I know my past and the past of those before my family is covered in sin. I seek your forgiveness please do not hold against my children the sins of those that come before them. In the name of Jesus, break any strongholds that are clinging to me and my family. I earnestly want my family to honor and serve you and your kingdom. May your mercy come quickly upon us. *Help us, God our Savior, for the glory of your name; deliver us and forgive our sins for your name's sake Psalm 79:9 (NIV).* We will praise your name forever and ever.

In Jesus's name,
Amen

*"Restore us, o God; make your face
shine on us, that we may be saved."*

Psalm 80:3

Dear God,

Hear me, Lord, restore my family. Make your face shine upon us that we may be saved. Help us to seek renewal and strength for each day by reading your Word daily and spending time alone with you. I pray my children will become connected to you and bear good fruit for your glory. As their mother and father, help us to stay connected to you so we will know how to raise our children according to your will. Show me what to pray for, when to become involved, what words to say when, so that my children may grow up experiencing your blessing.

In Jesus's name,
Amen

"If my people would only listen to me, if Israel would only follow my ways, how quickly I would subdue their enemies and turn my hand against their foes."

Psalm 81:13–14

Dear God,

I sing to you, God, my strength, for you are always here for me and my family. You provide comfort, guidance, mercy, forgiveness, and truth to us when we need it most. It can be so easy for us to create false idols out of things in this world. My prayer for my family is that you will convict our hearts when we start to worship anything other than you. Make it known to us what we are placing above you and point our hearts and desires back to you. I pray my children will listen to your commands and not follow the stubbornness of their own hearts. Let the blessings you pour out upon my children be used for your glory.

In Jesus's name,
Amen

"Defend the weak and the fatherless; uphold the cause of the poor and the oppressed. Rescue the weak and the needy; deliver them from the hand of the wicked."

Psalm 82:3–4

BUS STOP PRAYERS

Dear God,

I love you, dear Father, and give my broken self to you. Right now I feel a little lost, unsure of what to do or where you are leading me and my family. I know you are working in my heart, making changes, showing me things I used to ignore. I see that I am not fully giving myself to you and I am sorry. I feel as though you are placing more on my heart, especially regarding the weak, poor, and oppressed. I pray I can show my children how to live the way Jesus did and that I too will be more like Jesus. I praise your name and rejoice for you are good.

In Jesus's name,
Amen

"Let them know that you, whose name is the Lord—that you alone are the most high over all the earth."

Psalm 83:18

BUS STOP PRAYERS

Dear God,

I lift my children and the children of the coming generations up to you, mighty God. Create in them a heart for truth, a heart for Jesus. I pray they will fall in love with scripture. Bring us back to the Word and how beautiful it is on its own. Keep these children from following lies, but instead let them learn how to seek the truth. Your enemies are plotting ways to lead our children astray and it is with all my conviction that I lift up this prayer to you. Protect these children from the enemy and keep them on the path that leads into your loving arms. May one day everyone know you whose name is the Lord, that you alone are the most high over all the earth.

In Jesus's name,
Amen

"Blessed are those who dwell in your house; they are ever praising you."

Psalm 84:4

"Better is one day in your courts than a thousand elsewhere."

Psalm 84:10

Dear God,

Blessed is the one who trusts in you. May my children begin to trust in you from an early age. May they know you are their strength and the reason for any good thing they may have. May they praise your name all the days of their lives and never know what it is like to be without your unfailing love. I pray they never walk away from you, that they become so in love with you nothing else matters. Let this type of love come from the hearts of my children so they can pour out your love to everyone they meet. Forgive me when I doubt and feel this prayer to you seems impossible. I know in my heart you are good and I believe you will make this happen.

In Jesus's name,
Amen

*"You forgave the iniquity of your
people and covered all their sins."*

Psalm 85:2

*"Show us your unfailing love, Lord,
and grant us your salvation."*

Psalm 85:7

Dear God,

I praise you, Lord, for you are everything. You have shown mercy, grace, and forgiveness when it is not deserved. Despite all that we do wrong you still love us anyway. I pray that my children can show this type of love to everyone they meet. I can't even begin to express how amazed I am by the salvation you give each of us if we are willing to believe in your Son. Please bring my children to you and open their hearts to your Holy Spirit so they will receive the gift of salvation you have waiting for them. I pray they will listen to what you say and receive your promise of peace, that they will become faithful servants and not turn to foolishness.

> *Love and faithfulness meet together; righteousness and peace kiss each other. Faithfulness springs forth from the earth, and righteousness looks down from heaven. The Lord will indeed give what is good, and our land will yield its harvest. Righteousness goes before him and prepares the way for his steps Psalm 85:10-13 (NIV).*

The words above are my prayer for my children and for the generations to come. I pray they will be made righteous by Jesus, and that you will prepare the way for them to bring you glory and not miss your good and perfect plans. Never let anything keep my children from becoming who you created them to be.

In Jesus's name,
Amen

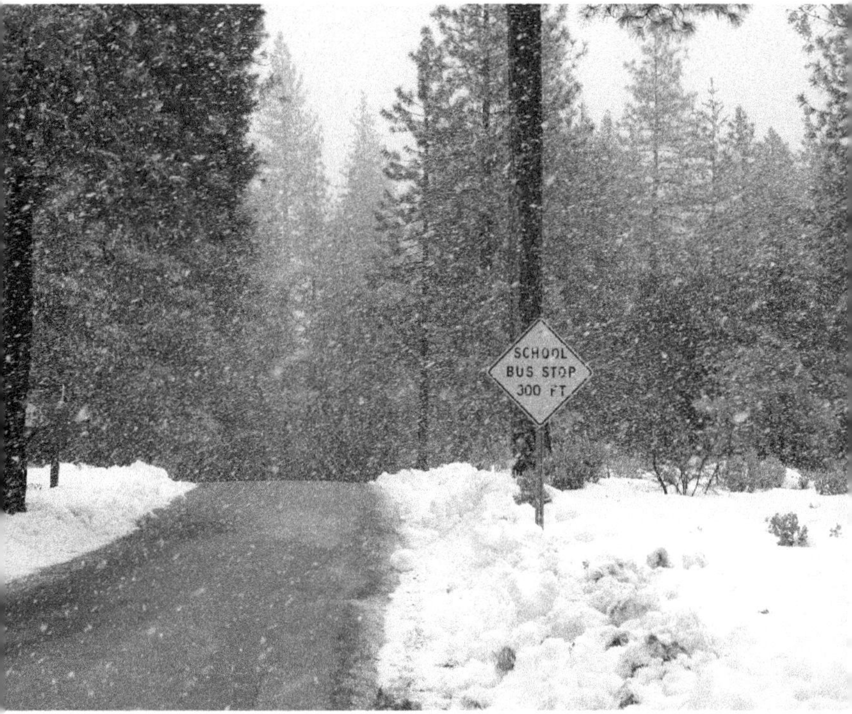
SCHOOL
BUS STOP
300 FT

"You, Lord, are forgiving and good, abounding in love to all who call to you. Hear my prayer Lord; listen to my cry for mercy. When I am in distress, I call to you because you answer me."

Psalm 86:5–7

Dear God,

I love you, Lord, with all my heart. I lift up these precious children to you, and pray for you to hear and answer these prayers I have written. My spirit feels weak at times and I am in need of you. Guard my life and the lives of my children and husband, for we have put our faith in you. Save them from this world and all of the ungodly things it can offer. You are my God, have mercy on me, oh Lord, for I do not always do what I should. I call to you all day long, for you to save my children, and their children, and their children's children, and so on. My dream is to one day witness my children being baptized and I give this prayer to you in trust. Let my children call your name and place their trust in you. Hear my prayer and have mercy upon me and my family. When I feel distressed, let me turn to you. There is no god like you, no deeds can compare to yours. *All the nations you have made will come and worship before you, Lord, they will bring glory to your name Psalm 86:9 (NIV).*

Let my children see you are great and do marvelous deeds, that you alone are God. Teach them your way, that they may rely on your faithfulness. Give my children an undivided heart that they may fear your name. I will praise you, Lord my God, with all my heart.

I will glorify your name forever and pray the generations after me will also.

You are compassionate and gracious, dear God, slow to anger and abounding in love and faithfulness Psalm 86:15 (NIV). Give my children a heart like Jesus and the desire to become more like you. Turn to my family and have mercy on us, show your strength and save my husband and children. Let them serve you to bring glory to your name. Give them a sign of your goodness, for I am so blessed that you, Lord, have helped me and comforted me as a wife and mother.

In Jesus's name,
Amen

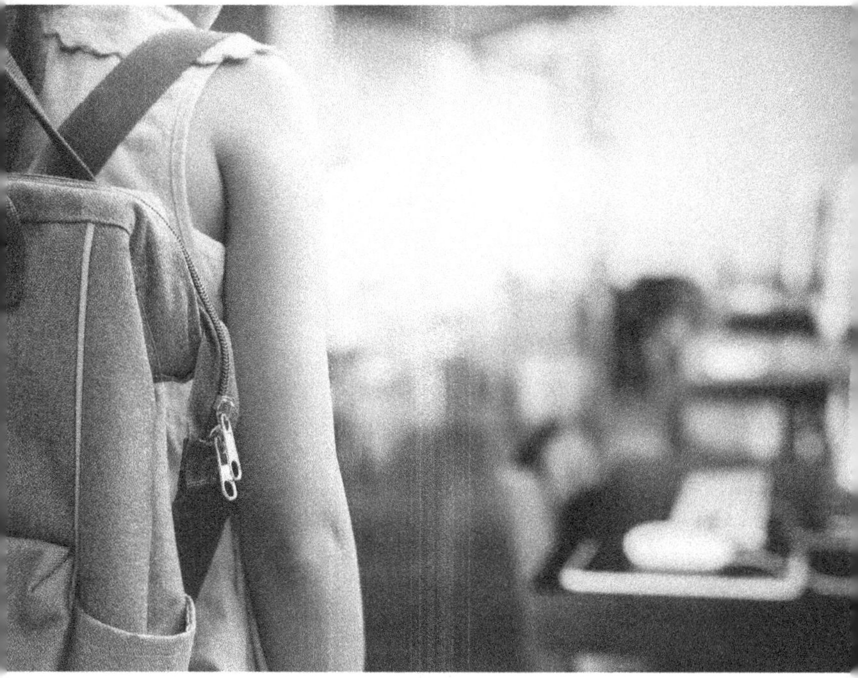

"I will sing of the Lord's great love forever; with my mouth I will make your faithfulness known through all generations. I will declare that your love stands firm forever, that you have established your faithfulness in heaven itself."

Psalm 89:1–2

Dear God,

You have entrusted me with these three precious lives. With you by my side I trust you to provide me with what I need each day to bring them closer to you. Help me declare that your love stands firm forever, that you have established your faithfulness in heaven itself. I pray my children will learn to praise your wonders, for nothing can compare to you and your faithfulness. Give my children your foundation of righteousness and justice, let your love and faithfulness go before them. Bless my children that they will choose to walk in the light of your presence, Lord, and rejoice in your name all day long. I pray they will celebrate your righteousness, for you are our glory and strength. As you did with your faithful chosen servant, David, I pray your hand will sustain and give strength to my children. Do not let the enemy get the better of them, or be oppressed by the wicked, but instead let your faithful love be with them, that they will bring a lifetime of glory to you. As their mother, I cry out to you, you are my Father, my rock, my Savior, hear my prayer, o Lord, and save my children and the next generations to come. Forgive us of our sins, I am truly sorry for the times we go against your commands and do not obey your call. Help

me and my family to be faithful, to serve, and love at all times. Praise be to the Lord forever!
In Jesus's name,
Amen

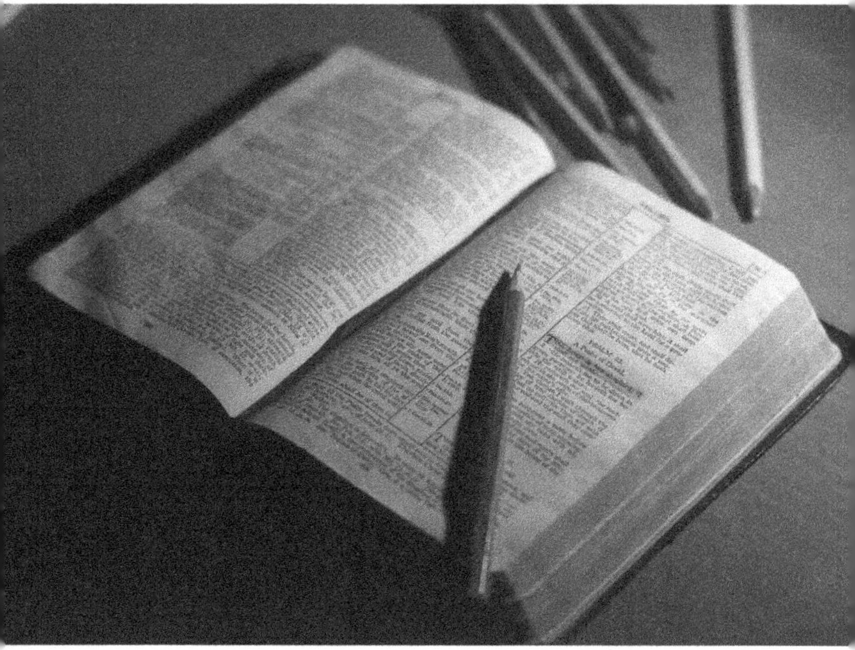

"Lord, you have been our dwelling place throughout all generations."

Psalm 90:1

"Teach us to number our days, that we may gain a heart of wisdom."

Psalm 90:12

"May your deeds be shown to your servants, your splendor to their children. May the favor of the Lord our God rest on us; establish the work of our hands for us—yes, establish the work of our hands."

Psalm 90:16–17

Dear God,

You are the God of all eternity. Forever you will stand righteous, holy, and perfect in all your loving ways. My heart is filled with the knowledge of your love and the awe of your glory. I have a hard time understanding at times why you chose us and continue to show your mercy, compassion, and love to us. I am so sorry for the hurt we cause, please forgive us. Thankful doesn't even come close to the way I feel when I think of your perfect plan for this world, your Son, our Savior. I am grateful for the knowledge of you, your Son, and your love, and I have always chosen you. I pray my children and my husband choose you, always. *Teach my children to number their days, that they may gain a heart of wisdom Psalm 90:12 (NIV)*. May your splendor be shown to my children and their hearts be grateful for each tiny detail, each blessing, you bestow upon them.

Establish the work of my mothering hands. May your work and love be brought forth from them.

In Jesus's name,
Amen

"Whoever dwells in the shelter of the most high will rest in the shadow of the almighty. I will say of the Lord, 'He is my refuge and my fortress, my God, in whom I trust.'"

Psalm 91:1–2

BUS STOP PRAYERS

Dear God,

Let my children pray, *You are my refuge, my fortress, my God, in whom I trust Psalm 91:1-2 (NIV)*. You are all these things to me as I grow in my relationship with you and slowly learn to give you more and more of my trust. Your word says, *Surely, he will save you from the fowler's snare, Psalm 91:3 (NIV)*. And I believe this to be true for my children. Save them so they will bring glory to you and you alone. *Under your wings let them find refuge, let your faithfulness be their shield Psalm 91:4 (NIV)*. Because of your promises, I am learning not to fear the night or the darkness of this world, but how to place my trust in you. I know these children are not mine, yet I cling to them and do not always give them or myself to you, foolishly thinking I can do more on my own, that my plans are better. Forgive me, dear Father! I know your plans are good and perfect. I pray for my grasp to loosen completely so I can wholeheartedly lift my children up to you. I am also learning not to fear that which can hurt my flesh, but that which can damage my soul and the souls of my family. We do not put you to the test, dear Lord, but trust your promise that when we place our faith in you, we are safe with you forever. If it is your will, I pray for a long life to watch my family grow and support them in their growth with you to witness the glorious plans you have for them. I pray I will witness their baptisms—

what a glorious day that will be! I love you, dear Father, I always have, and always will.

In Jesus's name,
Amen

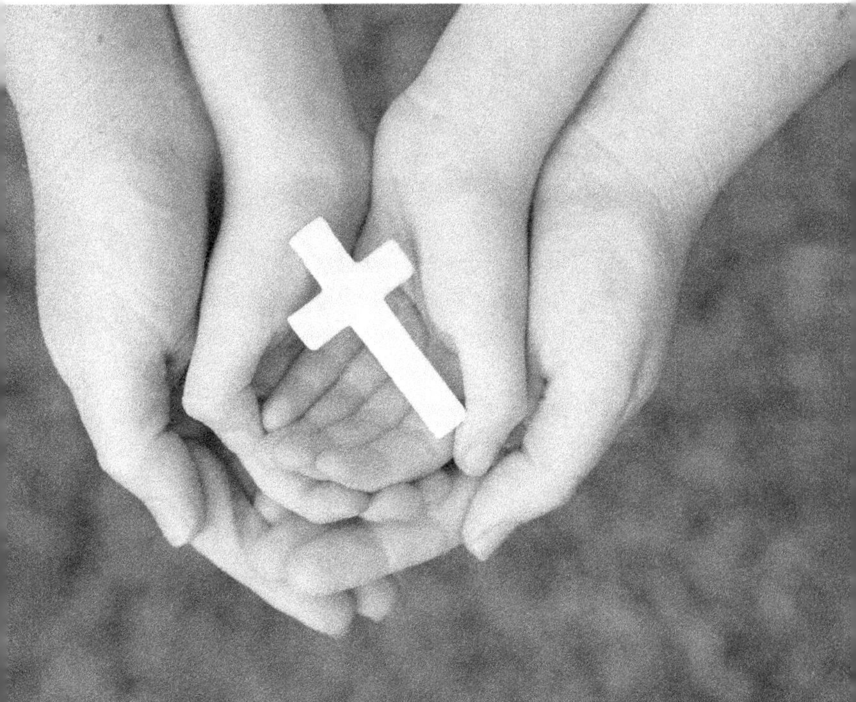

"…Planted in the house of the Lord, they will flourish in the courts of our God. They will still bear fruit in old age, they will stay fresh and green…"

Psalm 92:13–14

Dear God,

I pray my children see how good it is to praise your Name, dear Lord. Help them to learn to come to you first each morning and pray to you before they go to bed. I love you for who you are, Lord, not just for what you have done. Remind us each day that your thoughts are not like ours. Help us to be patient, and know that you are God, and we are not. I pray my children, covered in the righteousness of your Son, will flourish and grow strong in you, becoming exactly the person you created them to be. Let my children bear good fruit throughout their lives. May they believe, *The Lord is upright, he is my rock, and there is no wickedness in him Psalm 92:15 (NIV)*.

In Jesus's name,
Amen

"Your statutes, Lord, stand firm; holiness adorns your house for endless days."

Psalm 93:5

Dear God,

Your reign is from eternity, and how thankful I am for an unchanging God. I rest in the fact that your Word is forever. Your plan was perfect, even before creation, in your holiness. I place my trust in your mighty and loving hands. Thank you, Father, that we can come before you with our hearts, our praise, our fears, and our sin. In your unfailing love for us, you gave us Jesus. I pray my children and future generations will know this type of love.

In Jesus's name,
Amen

*"Blessed is the one you discipline,
Lord, the one you teach from
your law; you grant them relief
from days of trouble..."*

Psalm 94:12

Dear God,

My heart is filled with gladness and awe for the help you are waiting to give me each day as a mother to my children. Thank you for leading me to bring my children closer to building a relationship with you. I pray for continual guidance and wisdom when disciplining my children, and thank you, dear Father, for showing me the way to their hearts. Let my children choose wisdom over foolishness, choose you over distractions, and choose following your Word over following the world. Keep their hearts upright and filled with your Spirit. When one of my children was feeling anxious, you gave her peace and joy. Praise your holy name! Continue to show my children how to see you as their rock, their fortress, in whom to take refuge from the problems of this world.

In Jesus's name,
Amen

*"Come, let us bow down in worship,
let us kneel before the Lord our
maker; for he is our God and
we are the people of his pasture,
the flock under his care. Today,
if only you would hear his voice,
'Do not harden your hearts...'"*

Psalm 95:6–8

Dear God,

We give you our praises this morning, bringing you our hearts filled with the joy that can only come from you. Please let my children see that joy is not dependent upon our circumstances. What a gift this would be for them. We come before you with thanksgiving, for you always so freely pour out your goodness and love upon us. You are the great God, the great king above all gods. Your mighty hand brought life and everything in creation belongs to you. We are so small and broken, yet you choose to love us. I bow down on my knees to you, dear Father, in all of your glory. I pray my children will always make you their God forever and ever, that they will always be under your care. Let them hear your voice, even from a young age, and soften their hearts to your word and commands. Never let them stray. I need your help in teaching my children how to listen for you. Please show me how to grow submissive attitudes and obedient hearts in my children that they will be used for your glory.

In Jesus's name,
Amen

"Worship the Lord in the splendor of his holiness; tremble before him, all the earth."

Psalm 96:9

Dear God,

I proclaim your rightful place as the one, true God, and pray my children will be given the strength and courage to proclaim your truth to the world. I pray they begin to learn of your marvelous deeds and will share them with those you place in their path and to the next generations. You are great, o Lord, and worthy of praise. May my children fear your name. May they also proclaim your glory, strength, and holiness. *Let all creation rejoice before the Lord, for he comes Psalm 96:13 (NIV)*. And when that day arrives, let my children be wrapped in the righteousness of Jesus, your Son.

In Jesus's name,
Amen

*"Let those who love the Lord
hate evil, for he guards the lives
of his faithful ones and delivers
them from the hand of the wicked.
Light shines on the righteous and
joy on the upright in heart."*

Psalm 97:10–11

Dear God,

I pray my children will learn to appreciate your beautiful creation and how your glory, power, and love shine throughout all of the earth and into heaven. Let them be in awe of you. I pray they will pass down that admiration and love to their children and all of the generations to come. Keep my children from worshipping false idols, but instead I pray they will be given an undivided heart for you. Make them lovers of good and not evil. Guard their little lives with all you are, my Father, for they are so precious to me. I am nothing compared to how precious they must be in your sight. Fill their eyes with your light, their hearts with your joy, so that my children will draw others nearer to you.

We rejoice and praise your holy name.
In Jesus's name,
Amen

"The Lord has made his salvation known and revealed his righteousness to the nations."

Psalm 98:2

Dear God,

I thank you for the gift of my salvation. It is more precious to me than anything imaginable, knowing this perfect love that can only come from you. Lead my children and husband to accept this holy gift. Open their hearts to Jesus and the Gospel as truth and may they give thanks for their own salvation. Help me to fill my home with joy and praises for you and your goodness.
   In Jesus's name,
   Amen

"Let them praise your great and awesome name—he is holy."

Psalm 99:3

"...they called on the Lord and he answered them."

Psalm 99:6

Dear God,

I pray my children will fathom your greatness and be in awe of who you are. May they fear your name and be filled with genuine love for you and your Son. I pray they will call upon your holy name from the time they are small. I believe you will answer them just as you did with Samuel. When my children go against your commands, I pray they will be exposed right away, so they can learn valuable lessons and avoid years of heartache and trouble. We are blessed to be able to call upon you as our strength and shield. I praise you, Father, for you are good and holy.

In Jesus's name,
Amen

"For the Lord is good and his love endures forever; his faithfulness continues through all generations."

Psalm 100:5

BUS STOP PRAYERS

Dear God,

I know you are the one true God. May my lips and the lips of my husband and children speak your truth, shout for joy, and worship you with gladness. Transform our home to place of praise and joy for you. How blessed we are that you made us and we are yours. Before we present our requests and needs, let us come before you with thanksgiving and a heart ready to praise. May the love for you that has been in my heart since I was a young child be passed on to my children. By your grace may that love grow to be an even bigger and more trustworthy love than I could ever imagine. Let this love continue to be passed down throughout the generations to come.

Praise be to our Father!
In Jesus's name,
Amen

"I will conduct the affairs of my house with a blameless heart."

Psalm 101:2

Dear God,

Thank you, Lord, for who you are and that we are able to draw near to you. I sing of your love and justice in my heart as I write this, placing my trust and my faith in you to deliver my husband and children from this world and into your kingdom. As a mother it feels almost nearly impossible to keep my children's hearts, thoughts, and actions pure and in accordance to your will. *But I am sorry for my little faith. I know because your Word assures me that you are stronger than this world. Jesus has already defeated this world with his work on the cross, so my children can be covered in his righteousness and grow to be pure and godly in their hearts, thoughts, and actions.* The world leads me to think this is impossible—but I know better, because I am placing my faith in you, that your promises are true. I *need* your help, Father, to conduct the affairs of my household with a blameless heart, for alone, I fail miserably at this. Forgive me for my sin, cleanse me of the world, and lift me up as I follow you. I pray my children will look upon evil with disapproval. Keep them from becoming involved in what faithless people do, nor will they slander others or have haughty eyes and a proud heart. If those things ever begin to creep in, I pray you will make me and my husband aware and show us how to lead our children back to you and your ways. Set their eyes upon the faithful. Bring in family, friends, teachers, coaches, acquaintances, and the like who will lead our children closer to you. Let no one in my home practice dishonesty or tell lies, but instead give my family a heart for honesty and truth.

In Jesus's name,
Amen

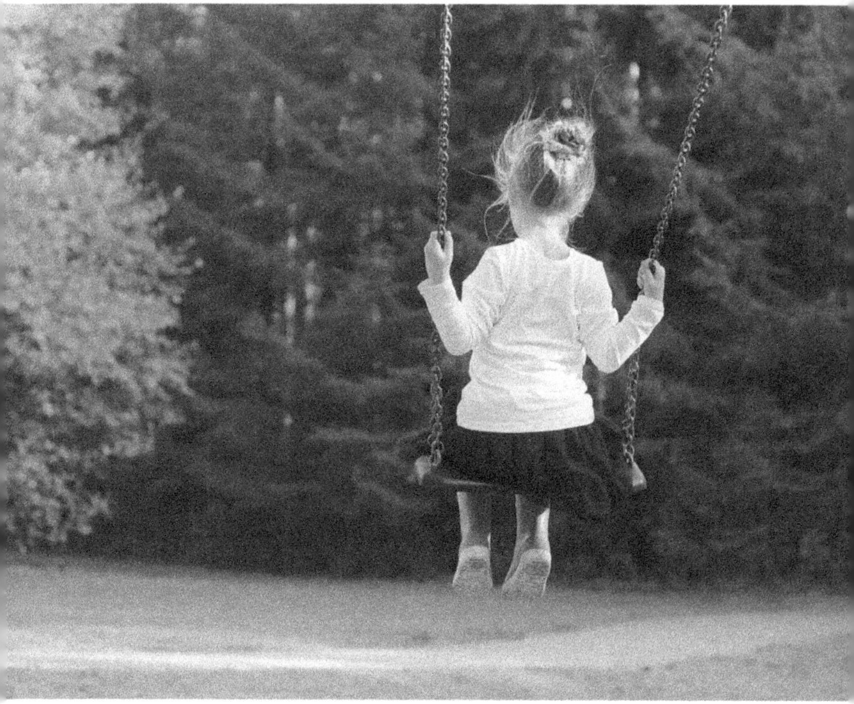

"Let this be written for a future generation, that a people not yet created may praise the Lord."

Psalm 102:18

"But you remain the same, and your years will never end. The children of your servants will live in your presence; their descendants will be established before you."

Psalm 102:27–28

Dear God,

How blessed we are, Father, that your compassion and mercies are new each morning. Help me to teach this to my children so their little hearts will learn your forgiveness and the beautiful love you have for us, even during difficult times. I believe you have placed upon my heart a deep desire to point my children and future generations to you and your Son. I pray every day that you will help me to seize those moments when I can use your Word and teachings to bring my children closer to you. You have given us the Word, so that we may tell of your great works and perfect love to our children and generations yet to be created, that they may praise your name. If it is your will, Father, I pray these scriptural prayers I am lifting up to you will be shared among those you have planned, and for those who read this will be surrounded by your presence and their hearts will be forever changed by you.

In Jesus's name,
Amen

"The Lord is compassionate and gracious, slow to anger, abounding in love. He does not treat us as our sins deserve or repay us according to our iniquities."

Psalm 103:8, 10

BUS STOP PRAYERS

Dear God,

May my children know in their heart how you are the one who forgives us of our sin, heals us from disease, redeems our lives from darkness, crowns us with love and compassion, satisfies our desires with good things, so that we can be made stronger in you *Psalm 103:3–5 (NIV)*. I pray my children will have eyes that see the oppressed around them and a heart that wants to serve you by helping. Give opportunities for my children to see your compassion and grace. May these qualities be emulated in my behavior as a mother to my children and in their behavior toward each other and their neighbor.

How thankful we are that you do not treat us as we deserve, but instead you chose to let your grace flow freely to us. *For as high as the heavens are above the earth, so great is his love for those who fear him; as far as the east is from the west, so far has he removed our transgressions from us Psalm 103:11–12 (NIV)*. My mind has a hard time wrapping around your immeasurable grace and love. I humble myself before you and stand in awe of who you are.

Your compassion is refreshing to me each morning. I pray my husband and I can show this compassion to our children. May they rejoice in the newness of each day you give. Change their hearts to truly care for others. I pray they will learn to put themselves last and not become obsessed with "self" as the world has become today. Open their eyes to their frailty so they understand from where they came and do not become proud or forget to keep their eyes on eternity with you. May your love be with our family each day and your righteousness with my children and their children's children that they will choose to keep and obey your commands.

With great joy and thanksgiving I lift up my praises to you, Father.

In Jesus's name,

Amen

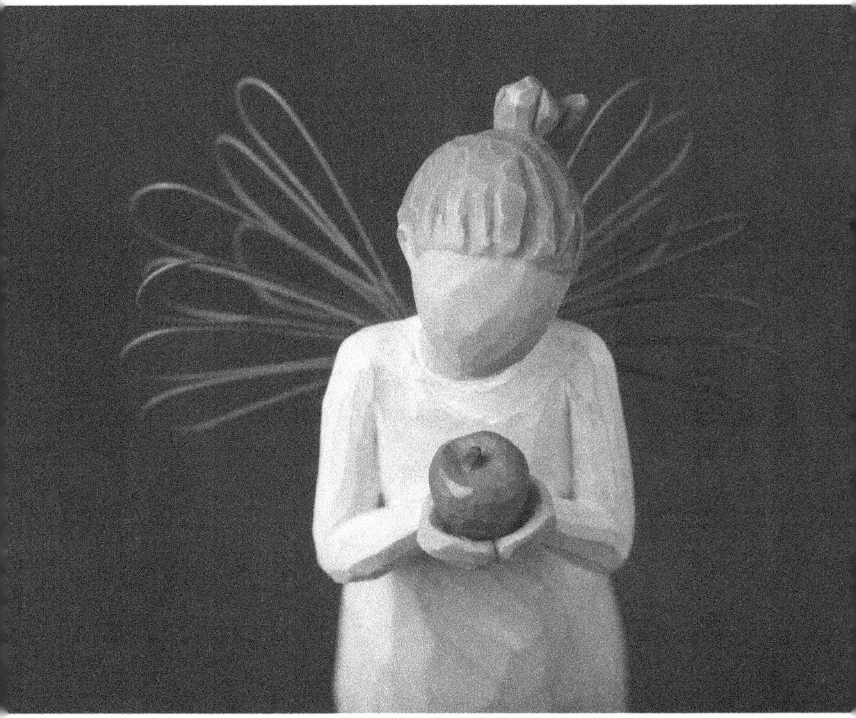

*"How many are your works, Lord!
In wisdom you made them all; the
earth is full of your creatures."*

Psalm 104:24

*"I will sing to the Lord all
my life, I will sing praise to
my God as long as I live."*

Psalm 104:33

Dear God,

Father, in your wisdom you created my precious children and entrusted them to me and my husband. I am forever grateful and thankful for the gift of motherhood. I want to raise my children with wisdom and pray they will grow to be wise and faithful followers of Jesus. Please pour out your wisdom and grace upon our family, for I know I will fail on my own.

Let us remember to look to you for help with patience and hope, for you give all creatures what they need at the proper time. Help me to remember to wait upon your timing with gladness and to place my trust in you. I pray my children will grow to display this quality in their own lives. May your glory endure forever and ever.

In Jesus's name,
Amen

*"He remembers his covenant
forever, the promise he made,
for a thousand generations."*

Psalm 105:8

Dear God,

You are the one true God, our Father, and we praise your holy name this morning. Use me and my children to make known among the nations what you have done, in whatever form that may be. I love to hear my children sing your name as we listen to the radio in the car on our way here and there. I pray if it is your will they will have a heart for music and use song to worship and bring glory to you. It is my prayer this day that my children and the children of the current and future generations will, *Look to the Lord and his strength; and seek his face always Psalm 105:4 (NIV)*. Each day let us remember the wonders you have done and pass on those miracles and judgments to the next generation. Help me to teach my children your promises and how you are always faithful to keep each one. May my children keep your teaching and observe your laws with a joyful heart.

Praise be to the Lord.
In Jesus's name,
Amen

*"Blessed are those who act justly,
who always do what is right."*

Psalm 106:3

*"Many times he delivered them,
but they were bent on rebellion and
they wasted away in their sin."*

Psalm 106:43

Dear God,

With a sincere heart I give thanks to the Lord for he is good, *his love endures forever Psalm 106:1 (NIV)*. Bless my children with your love and lead their hearts to act justly, to want to do what is right. When they sin before you, may my children come to you right away and seek forgiveness.

Remember me and my family, Lord, and include us in your great mercies. I know we have sinned and acted wrongly. Forgive us and help us to fully repent from our sinful ways. You have blessed us with more than we could ever imagine. We have enjoyed wonderful and loving times as a family because of your generous hand. I pray that my children will not look to you only during hard times. May they never forget your mercies or stop seeking your face during the "good times" in their lives. Give your wisdom to my children and a yearning for knowing you more. It can be so hard to wait patiently for your plan to unfold. Bestow upon my children a heart of patience that wants to please you and do your will. Keep my children from giving in to their cravings or putting you to the test. May they be so filled with your wisdom they will never exchange their glorious God for a worthless idol. May they never forget the God who has the power to save them, to give them the gift of eternal life. Use me and my husband, family, friends, and teachers to help keep their hearts from rebellion against the Spirit of God. Save my children and the current and future generations. *Gather them from the nations, that we may give thanks to your holy name and glory in your praise. Praise be to the Lord, the God of Israel, from everlasting to everlasting Psalm 106:47–48, (NIV).*

Let all the people say, "Amen!" Praise the Lord Psalm 106:48 (NIV).

In Jesus's name,
Amen

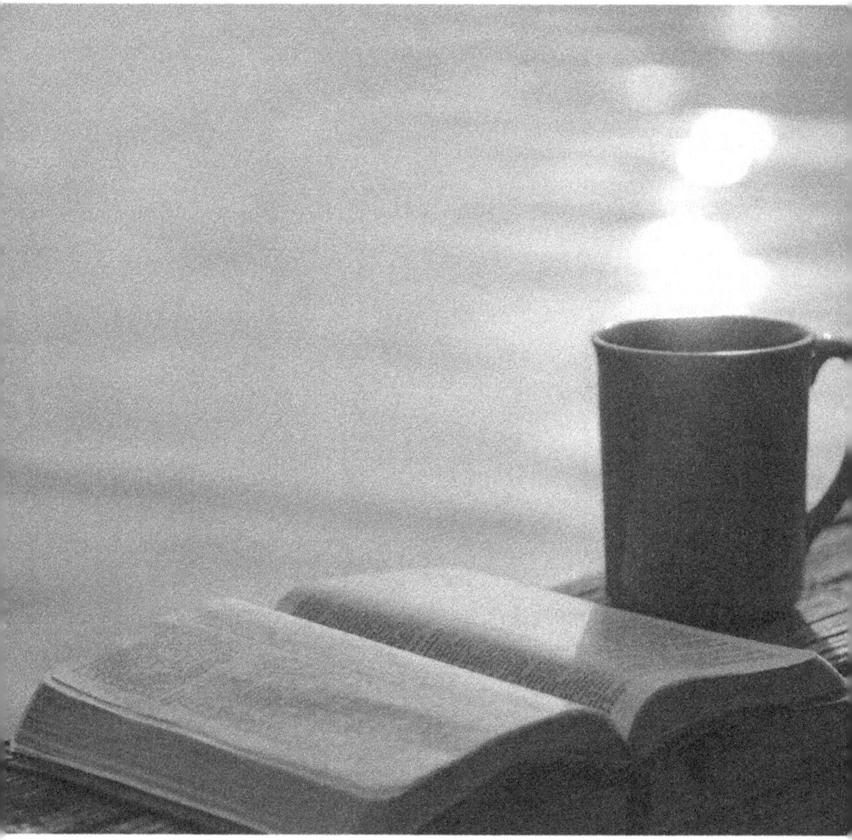

"Then they cried to the Lord in their trouble, and he saved them from their distress."

Psalm 107:13

"He sent out his word and healed them; he rescued them from the grave."

Psalm 107:20

Dear God,

My heart comes to you filled with thankfulness, for who you are, not for what you do. I love you, Father. I pray my children will love you in return of the great love you bestow upon them. When they are thirsty and hungry, I pray they come to you first to meet their needs. May their hearts be so filled with your love that they never despise your commands. Forgive me for taking for granted your unfailing love and how you are always there to rescue me from trouble. I pray my children will grow up with an appreciation for not only your great works, but for how much you truly love us.

Let your wisdom come upon my children and my family that we may use it for your glory.

In Jesus's name,
Amen

*"For great is your love, higher
than the heavens; Your faithfulness
reaches to the skies."*

Psalm 108:4

*"With God we will gain the
victory, and he will trample
down our enemies."*

Psalm 108:13

Dear God,

I bring my praise and love to you this morning, Father, for you are everything to me. I am so thankful for the time I am able to spend with you in prayer. Your love is beyond measure. I pray for you to grow a steadfast heart of faith and love in my family, dear Lord, that we may glorify your name and be a blessing to others.

Save us and help us with your right hand that those you love may be delivered Psalm 108:6 (NIV). Let my family see that everything good comes from you. Apart from you we have nothing. I give you my heart as a mother and the hearts of my family for you to shape and soften so they can be used for your great purpose. With you, Father, I am certain my children will have victory over the world.

In Jesus's name,
Amen

"The fear of the Lord is the beginning of wisdom."

Psalm 111:10

Dear God,

My heart has loved you since I can remember. I have always loved to praise your name. I have always loved to hear about your works, commands, grace, power, and compassion. Let this love I have for you overflow into my family and to everyone I see. I pray my children will have this same love and desire for you and your Word from a young age and that it will never stop growing. Forgive me of my current and past sins, and let my children not suffer from my mistakes, but instead they will be blessed by you and grow in wisdom. Help me and my husband guide our children to you.

To you, Father, we praise your holy and awesome name.

In Jesus's name,
Amen

"Blessed are those who fear the Lord, who find great delight in his commands. Their children will be mighty in the land; the generation of the upright will be blessed."

Psalm 112:1–2

BUS STOP PRAYERS

Dear God,

I lift up the hearts of my children, that your holy presence will fill them as they go about their day. One area of their heart, which I know can be hard, is the act of giving generously and freely. Give me the strength and wisdom to teach my children how to live with open hands, knowing everything they have belongs to you and is to be used for your glory. We really struggle with this at times, and I give this area to you to work in us and grow us. I pray my children's hearts will become steadfast and trusting in you, that they will have no fear, as they give lovingly and freely to others. Thank you for the gift of your Word, which brings upon my heart ways to help our family become all that you created us to be.

In Jesus's name,
Amen

"From the rising of the sun to the place where it sets, the name of the Lord is to be praised."

Psalm 113:3

BUS STOP PRAYERS

Dear God,

We have enjoyed so many sunrises and sunsets in the home you gave us. I am thankful for each day I am given—even for the hard ones. Let the hearts of my children learn how to see each day as a gift from you, and to use that day wisely in a way that helps those in need and serves you. Never let them become proud or think they are above anyone, for you exalt the lowly.

There is nothing that could ever compare to you and your goodness, Father.

In Jesus's name,
Amen

"Not to us, Lord, not to us but to your name be the glory, because of your love and faithfulness."

Psalm 115:1

Dear God,

Humble my children that they will learn to say, "Not to me, not to me, but to God be the glory." You have given them each their own special gifts and talents, and I pray with my whole heart that they will never be afraid to speak your name to give you the glory for all they accomplish. May they never rest thinking it was because of their own efforts or give the praise to anything but you.

How thankful I am, Father, that you are my help and my shield to go through this experience of raising children. Thank you that among all of your greatness, you remember me, my husband, and my children, and that you bless us. Help me and my husband continually seek your face and grow in you, that our family may flourish.

Praise be to your name.
In Jesus's name,
Amen

"I will lift up the cup of salvation and call on the name of the Lord."

Psalm 116:13

"Truly I am your servant, Lord; I serve you just as my mother did; you have freed me from my chains."

Psalm 116:16

Dear God,

How thankful my heart is, Father, for you always hear my voice. More times than I can count, you have answered me in your own perfect way. I know my children are trying to understand how you can hear them and how they can begin to hear you. It is my prayer that you will grow this desire to communicate with you and to begin a loving relationship that will thrive their entire lives. So many times your graciousness and compassion have saved me. I pray that I will remember to rest my soul knowing you have been so good to me and my family.

Most of all, I give thanks to you for my salvation, for it is everything I have. Please, Father, bring your Holy Spirit upon my husband, and my children, that they will one day accept your treasured gift of salvation.

I give my heart to you, filled with joy and thanksgiving.

In Jesus's name,
Amen

"For great is his love toward us, and the faithfulness of the Lord endures forever."

Psalm 117:2

Dear God,

It is such a blessing to come to you and simply praise your name. Thank you for choosing to love us in all of your great faithfulness. May my family always choose to love you first.

I love you, heavenly Father, for who you are.

In Jesus's name,
Amen

"The Lord is with me; I will not be afraid. What can mere mortals do to me? The Lord is with me; he is my helper."

Psalm 118:6–7

Dear God,

I awake with thankfulness in my heart. I pray my children will see how you are good and how your love endures forever. When they go through hard times, I pray they take refuge in you first and come to trust in you.

I am also thankful for the times you have given me refuge in the trials of motherhood, when I have felt surrounded on every side and about to fall. I remembered to call on you and you helped me. Let this be my prayer also, that I will always remember to seek you first in my own trials and rely on your strength, not my own.

Lord, you are my God, and I pray you will let your light shine on us.

In Jesus's name,
Amen

"I call with all my heart; answer me, Lord, and I will obey your decrees. I call out to you; save me and I will keep your statutes. I rise before dawn and cry for help; I have put my hope in your word. My eyes stay open through the watches of the night, that I may meditate on your promises. Hear my voice in accordance with your love; preserve my life, Lord, according to your laws. Those who devise wicked schemes are near, but they are far from your law. Yet you are near, Lord, and all of your commands are true."

Psalm 119:145–151

Dear God,

I thank you for another day to be a mother to my beautiful children, dear Lord. I love you with my entire heart. I lift up my children and all of the children in the world, that they will be blameless in your sight for the coming of Christ Jesus. I pray they will want to keep your commands, seek you with all of their heart, and follow you in all of your ways, not just when it is convenient. That is where I struggle, Lord, and I pray you will grow this part of me (and my husband) to follow you even when it is hard so we can be an example to our children.

I look down the road to when they are teenagers and beyond, and I begin to worry about their purity and feel disheartened by what I see around me. But I refuse to believe the lies of this world, and I know with all my heart when I call on the name of Jesus he will answer. Let my children live according to your holy Word, so they will remain pure for their future spouse. I pray their future spouse will also remain pure and connected to you. Do not let my children stray from your commands. Help my husband and me to always know when to correct our children and guide them to you. May our home, church, and surroundings be a place where my children can learn to hide your Word in their hearts, so they will not sin against you. I pray they will rejoice in you over and above any riches they may own. May they know all they are given is because of you and your great mercy. Teach me ways to show my children how to meditate on your Word from a young age so they will carry this skill with them for the rest of their lives.

Open their eyes to your great works that surround them each day. May they delight in you for who you are and may their hearts belong to heaven. Let them be consumed by you and not of this world, nor may they become arrogant, proud, or selfish. Give us strength, Lord, to do all you ask of our family. May your unfailing love come to my children and husband, your salvation, according to your promise. Then my children can answer anyone who taunts them for they trust in your word. Let my children understand that your commands will set them free, not hold them back.

When they endure trials, I pray they look to you as their comfort. Your promise preserves their lives. Even when others are mocking them for their faith in you, do not let them turn from your law.

Let them seek you with all their heart, turning their steps to you without delay. Teach them good judgment, for you are good and everything you do is good. As they begin and end each day, let it be with your name in their prayers.

Father, your hands created my children. Give them understanding to obey your commands, for they belong to you. Let your compassion come to my children that they might live.

In Jesus's name,
Amen

*"May my cry come before you,
Lord; give me understanding
according to your word. May my
supplication come before you; deliver
me according to your promise. May
my lips overflow with praise, for
you teach me your decrees. May my
tongue sing of your word, for all
your commands are righteous. May
your hand be ready to help me, for I
have chosen your precepts. I long for
your salvation, Lord, and your law
gives me delight. Let me live that I
may praise you, and may your laws
sustain me. I have strayed like a
lost sheep, Seek your servant, for I
have not forgotten your commands."*

Psalm 119:169–176

Dear God,

Thank you for your eternal word. It stands firm in the heavens forever. My hopeful prayer once again is that your faithfulness will be known through all the future generations. Save my children and all children, for they are yours. When I am feeling overwhelmed, like most days as a mother to young children, help me to remember you have no limits, o Lord. Your strength endures forever. Please help me to stay connected to you so I can fulfill the role of wife and mother that you have so graciously given me.

Our children belong to you. I pray for each child to receive your wisdom. Let your guidance keep them away from evil paths. May they see your Word as sweeter than honey, as a lamp to their feet, and light to their path. Let them learn to look to you for sustenance, to fear your name, and stand in awe of you. Make your face shine upon my children and all children, so this light may be seen by others. When they do wrong, let them feel remorse and want to turn to you for forgiveness.

Help me teach my children to begin their day with you, that you will hear their call. I pray they allow this communication to continue from morning to noon and into the night. Let them make time to meditate upon your word.

May they know you are always near and that you never leave their side.

As their mother, may my cry come before you, Lord, give me understanding according to your word. May my supplication come before you, deliver my children and husband according to your promises.

May praise always be upon my lips and my tongue sing of your love to my children. May your hand be ready to help me for I have chosen you above all else.

I long for your salvation for my children and husband, and your law gives me delight. Let me live that I may praise you and see my children's children. May your law sustain me and my family. When I stray, which I sometimes do, bring me and my family back to you, for love for you and the Son is always upon our hearts.

In Jesus's name,
Amen

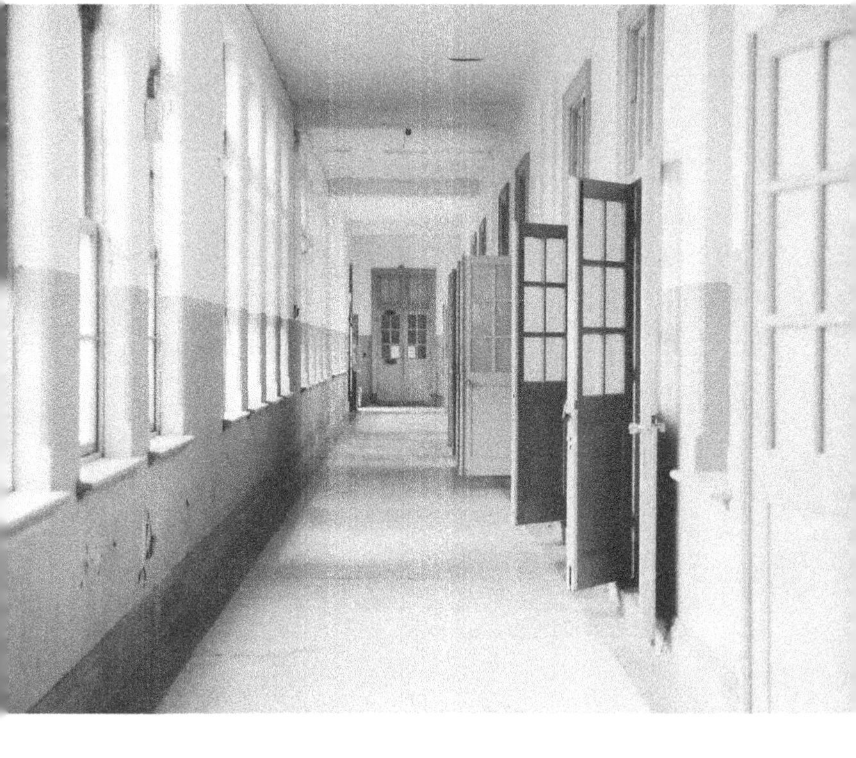

*"Save me, Lord, from lying lips
and from deceitful tongues."*

Psalm 120:2

Dear God,

How grateful I am that Jesus is the way, the truth and the life *John 14:6 (NIV)*. I pray my children will know the truth of your Son, that you will save them from the lies of this world. Grow courage in their hearts, to seek out the truth by measuring everything against your Word, and to speak your truth to others. I know with you, Lord, all things are possible.

In Jesus's name,
Amen

*"The Lord will watch over
your coming and going both
now and forevermore."*

Psalm 121:8

Dear God,

I am so blessed to come to you, the maker of heaven and earth, knowing you are my help. Guide our footsteps as mother and father, and those precious little steps of our children. I take comfort knowing it is you, Lord, who watches over me and my family. Give me eyes to see and ears to hear when you are speaking to me about my family, so that I may do what is right. You truly have been the shade at our right hand. Nothing has harmed us, and only because of you and your grace. Thank you for watching over us, keeping us in your loving arms.

In Jesus's name,
Amen

"…So our eyes look to the Lord our God, till he shows us his mercy."

Psalm 123:2

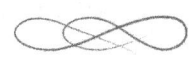

Dear God,

I pray that our eyes will be set on you, this day, and each day forward. Help us to fix our eyes on the cross, knowing you are with us and that you have mercy on us. Show me where and when to remove distractions from our lives and our homes, so that I can teach my children how to stay focused on you. I pray this for myself and my husband as well. Place on our hearts to not love those things that take us away from time with you. Replace those desires with the desire for growing closer to you.

Thank you, Father, for your love, grace, and work in our lives.

In Jesus's name,
Amen

"Those who sow with tears will reap with songs of joy. Those who go out weeping, carrying seed to sow, will return with songs of joy, carrying sheaves with them."

Psalm 126:5–6

Dear God,

You have shown me as I read your Word and write this prayer, that I am sowing seeds in my children's heart. I am planting your Word so that they may one day grow and bear much fruit for your glory. Today I worked on planting my seeds while in tears, feeling defeated and overwhelmed. But now I see and take comfort in knowing that even when I am having "one of those days," my seeds will one day grow into a joyful harvest.

I am forever grateful for your love.
In Jesus's name,
Amen

"Unless the Lord builds the house, the builders labor in vain. Unless the Lord watches over the city, the guards stand watch in vain."

Psalm 127:1

"Children are a heritage from the Lord, offspring a reward from him. Like arrows in the hands of a warrior are the children born in one's youth."

Psalm 127:3–4

Dear God,

Nothing good that I do as a wife or mother is because of my own achievement. I have come to learn this and thank you for making me humble. I pray, Father, that our home and my family will be built and grown by you. Please remind me when I am working in vain of the glory above, and that nothing will be as good as the plans you have for us. Fill our home with your Holy Spirit so we may be guided to you each day. I pray these words because I truly recognize how our children are a heritage from you. I want nothing more than for my children to follow you and be used for your glory. You have put this on my heart from a young age. I pray that I will please you since you have entrusted me with these three precious, amazing little lives.

In Jesus's name,
Amen

*"Blessed are all who fear the Lord,
who walk in obedience to him. You
will eat the fruit of your labor;
blessings and prosperity will be yours.
Your wife will be like the fruitful
vine within your house; your children
will be like olive shoots around your
table. Yes, this will be the blessing
for the man who fears the Lord."*

Psalm 128:1–4

Dear God,

May my children and husband grow to fear your name and walk in obedience to you. I pray I will also walk in obedience to you, so that one day we can eat the fruit of our labor. Make me into a fruitful vine within our home and my children like olive shoots around our table. May my husband fear your name and grow in his understanding. If it is your will, I pray my husband and I will live to see our children's children. What a joy! I can only imagine.

Thank you, Father, for your grace and for the guidance of your Word.

In Jesus's name,
Amen

"I wait for the Lord, my whole being waits, and in his word I put my hope. I wait for the Lord more than watchmen wait for the morning, more than watchmen wait for the morning."

Psalm 130:5–6

BUS STOP PRAYERS

Dear God,

How grateful and in awe I am for your forgiveness of our sins, so that we may serve you, our Lord and Savior. In your Word, Father, I have put my hope—my hope that one day my husband and children will come to you and receive your salvation. Until that day, my whole being waits for the Lord, for with you is unfailing love and full redemption.
In Jesus's name,
Amen

*"My heart is not proud, Lord,
my eyes are not haughty."*

Psalm 131:1

Dear God,

I pray for the hearts of my children, that they may never grow proud. Teach them to calm and quiet their souls, and be content knowing they are surrounded by you. May my husband and I grow to be an example of this practice. I know this can only be done with your help. I humble myself and my family before you that you may work in us.
In Jesus's name,
Amen

*"How good and pleasant it is when
God's people live together in unity!"*

Psalm 133:1

Dear God,

I continue to be amazed at how your Word is always perfect for the situations we are in. As a mother, it seems as though there are more times when my children are not living together in peace and unity. I feel so refreshed when I read, "How good and pleasant it is when God's people live together in unity!" I pray these words for my children and lift up their relationship as brothers and sister to you. Let them grow in unity, strengthening their bond by your grace. I pray they will remain close and take care of each other their entire lives. I pray they enjoy each other's company and will continually show each other love, even through the hard times. They are such blessings to each other. Do not let this world affect what you created in them. May they see each other as a gift from you that is to be cherished and loved.

In Jesus's name,
Amen

"Your name, Lord, endures forever, your renown, Lord, through all generations."

Psalm 135:13

Dear God,

Father, thank you for the ability to praise your name each day. We love you, humble ourselves before you, and give you complete control over ourselves and what happens to us today. We do this knowing that you are good and know what is best for us and your kingdom.
In Jesus's name,
Amen

"Give thanks to the Lord, for he is good, his love endures forever."

Psalm 136:1

Dear God,

I am truly thankful you are my heavenly Father, who loved us all so much that you gave your one and only Son that we may live with you forever. Thank you for cultivating a thankful heart in me. I see how much this practice of thanksgiving grows my faith and brings me closer to you. I give to you the hearts of my children, for at times it can be hard for them to truly be thankful in all circumstances. Do not let the empty promises of this world entice their hearts, but instead may they grow to cherish you and be thankful for each and every moment, blessing, and circumstance that is given by you. Grow contentment in their hearts. Show my husband and me ways to help this along. Give us strength when we are tired to do the work that truly matters—raising our children to live for you.

I give thanks to the Lord for he is good, his love endures forever Psalm 136:1 (NIV).

In Jesus's name,
Amen

*"When I called, you answered me;
you greatly emboldened me."*

Psalm 138:3

Dear God,

I praise you, Lord, with all my heart and give you thanks for this day with my children. Each day I face so many challenges. Each time I call out to you, you are faithful to answer in your own, loving way. Though I am nothing, you still look fondly upon me and my family, and for this I am in awe. I take comfort knowing when we are in trouble, you save us with your right hand. My faith has grown during these times and for that I am thankful. Please continue to grow us, forgive us of our sin, and with your blessing may we become what you created us to be.

In Jesus's name,
Amen

*"You have searched me, Lord,
and you know me."*

Psalm 139:1

*"For you created my inmost
being; you knit me together in
my mother's womb. I praise
you because I am fearfully and
wonderfully made; your works are
wonderful, I know that full well."*

Psalm 139:13–14

*"Search me, God, and know
my heart; test me and know my
anxious thoughts. See if there
is any offensive way in me, and
lead me in the way everlasting."*

Psalm 139:23–24

Dear God,

I rejoice in your Word, which reassures me of your greatness and love. Like the Psalmist, I too cannot begin to comprehend your ways. *You know me better than I know myself, which also means you know my children better than I could even begin to know them. This gives me such peace and I ask that you will open my eyes to the innermost thoughts and abilities of my children that I can, through your help, bring out their true, godly self, so they will become exactly who you created them to be.* It would pain my heart to see them wander from you and your will, for I know that the center of your will is the best place for them to be. I pray they know who they are—your child—from a young age. Never let them escape your loving hands. Keep them close to you.

You fearfully and wonderfully created these beautiful children inside of me, knitting them together, where nothing was hidden from you Psalm 139:13-14 (NIV). I know you placed special gifts and abilities inside my children. I have been given the desire to bring out and refine these treasures, so they may bring you glory. Search me and my family, dear Father, and know our hearts. Test us and know our anxious thoughts, show us any offensive ways in us and I pray we will repent and be led to the way everlasting.

In Jesus's name,
Amen

"Keep me safe, Lord, from the hands of the wicked; protect me from the violent, who devise ways to trip my feet."

Psalm 140:4

Dear God,

You know me, Father, and my heart. Now I lay at your feet my fear for the future of my children, especially when they are teenagers and young adults. I pray they are not enticed by the world and its wickedness and lies. Bless them with friends who are chosen by you for their good. Bring them friends that will help them in their walk with you, not lead them astray. You are my God, hear my prayer and protect the hearts of my children when my husband and I can't be there to speak your truth and keep their feet from tripping. Guide them in your infinite wisdom, love, and grace.

I am so blessed as a mother to know you and call on your name, my strong deliverer.

In Jesus's name,
Amen

"May my prayer be set before you like incense; may the lifting up of my hands be like the evening sacrifice."

Psalm 141:2

"But my eyes are fixed on you, sovereign Lord; in you I take refuge—do not give me over to death."

Psalm 141:8

BUS STOP PRAYERS

Dear God,

I lift my heart and hands to you, Lord, with all that I am. I offer you my prayers with true sincerity for the intercession of my children and the future generations. I love you and feel the thankfulness for your grace overflowing in my heart. Thank you for your Word, which gives me guidance as a wife and mother. It is where I love to turn in times of joy and sorrow and everything in between.

I pray for my children that you will set a guard over their mouths, Lord. Help them to keep watch over the door of their lips. I know this will take time. I ask for your wisdom as I help them with this each day. I need your loving Spirit to soften their hearts to each other.

Fix our eyes on you, Lord. Keep my family faithful to you and your kingdom.

In Jesus's name,
Amen

"When my spirit grows faint within me, it is you who watch over my way."

Psalm 142:3

Dear God,

What a beautiful example of your compassion you gave me today. When my spirit was feeling weak and wondering if I am doing anything right as a parent, you lifted me out of my despair by giving me the most wonderful joy found in the smallest moments with my children. When I seek constant communication with you through prayer and my Bible, I see how my day changes when your presence is invited. I begin to hear your prompting, feel your peace, and see your work.

Some days I feel the challenges that pursue me are too strong for me to bear. It is then I remember you are with me, waiting for my humble cry. Help me to share this goodness and strength you give me with other mothers, fathers, and caregivers, that I may bring them closer to you.

Thank you, Father, for the immense grace you give me each day.

In Jesus's name,
Amen

*"Let the morning bring me
word of your unfailing love,
for I have put my trust in you.
Show me the way I should go,
for to you I entrust my life."*

Psalm 143:8

Dear God,

I entrust this day to you, to do your loving and faithful work in the lives of my children. With each step they take, let it lead them to growing into a deeper relationship with you. Help us to remember to meditate on your Word by taking advantage of moments that become available. Let me be an example to my children in this way. Give us the strength to have the discipline it takes to not become caught up in the electronic world to quench our thirst for satisfaction, but instead teach my children to turn to you and the good things that are alive in this world you created. I feel surrounded by a changing culture that is looking to live in this artificial world. I feel your call to lead my family away from this and to keep our eyes on you and the life you created around us. This seems to be one of many challenges facing me as a parent. I know nothing is impossible for you and so I lay this concern at your feet.

In Jesus's name,
Amen

"He is my loving God and my fortress, my stronghold and my deliverer, my shield, in whom I take refuge."

Psalm 144:2

"Then our sons in their youth will be like well-nurtured plants, and our daughters will be like pillars carved to adorn a palace."

Psalm 144:12

Dear God,

Praise be to the Lord, my rock, who trains my motherly hands to take on the challenges of this day. By giving this day to you, I feel prepared and at peace. I love you and remain in awe that you care for me. Deliver my children from all who are against you so that my sons will be like well-nurtured plants and my daughter like a pillar. I pray that they will grow to bring glory to your name.

In Jesus's name,
Amen

"One generation commends your works to another; they tell of your mighty acts. They speak of the glorious splendor of your majesty—and I will meditate on your wonderful works. They tell the power of your awesome works—and I will proclaim your great deeds. They celebrate your abundant goodness and joyfully sing of your righteousness."

Psalm 145:4–7

Dear God,

I love to praise your name, ever since I can remember. I will continue to praise your holy name each day I am given. I have learned of your great works and how your Word remains unchanging and true forever. Fulfill my deep desire to share your works with my children and the future generations, in hopes they will continue to teach their children of your glorious splendor.

I pray as my children and all children grow, they will come to know who you are:

> *Gracious, compassionate, slow to anger, rich in love, good to all, compassionate on all you have made, trustworthy in your promises, faithful in all you do, uphold all who fall, lift up all who are bowed down, providing everything we need in your own perfect will, righteous, fulfills the desires of those who fear him, hears our cry and saves us, watches over all who love him, near to all who call on him in truth Psalm 145:8-20 (NIV).*

I pray they see your works for what they are: telling of the glory of your kingdom, speaking your might, how your kingdom is everlasting and your dominion endures forever.

May glory be to your name.
In Jesus's name,
Amen

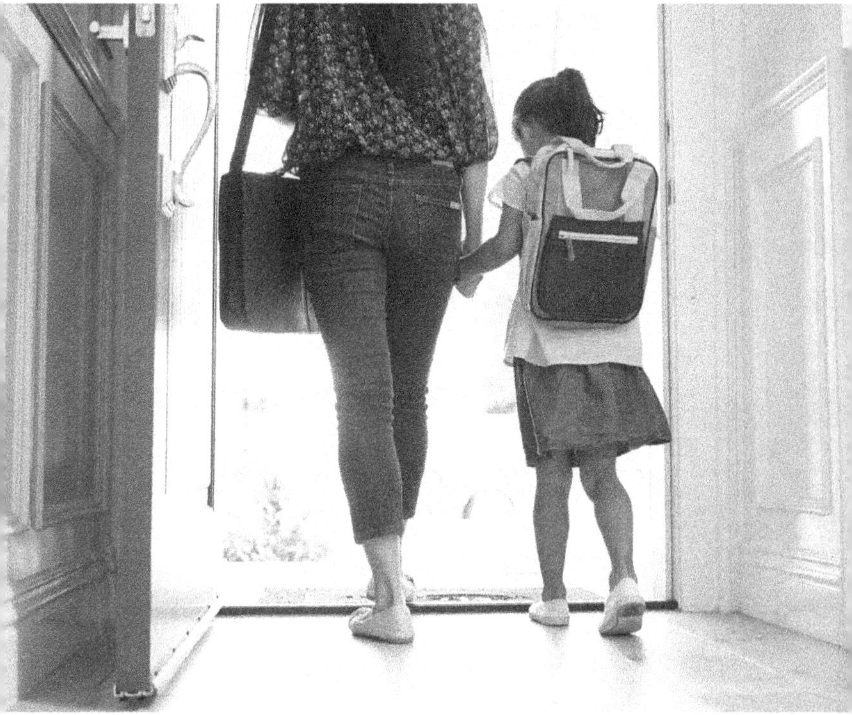

"He is the maker of heaven and earth, the sea, and everything in them—he remains faithful forever."

Psalm 146:6

Dear God,

I pray you will make your presence and power known in the lives of my children this day. I have come to understand so much of what they will do is based on what they see in me, my husband, and those close to them. I humbly ask for you to work in me and those close to my children by making Jesus real in our words and visible in our actions. Help my children surrender to you, in full trust. Give them a heart for the weak, oppressed, hungry, fatherless, widows, and all those who are in need of your love. I pray they grow up knowing how to serve and humble themselves before you and others.

In Jesus's name,
Amen

"His pleasure is not in the strength of the horse, nor his delight in the legs of the warrior; the Lord delights in those who fear him, who put their hope in his unfailing love."

Psalm 147:10–11

Dear God,

How good it is to praise your name and humble myself before you. I love to read how you heal the brokenhearted, determine the number of stars, and call them each by name, cover the sky with clouds, supply the earth with rain, make grass grow on the hills, and provide for each living creation. Yet your pleasure is not in greatness, it is in those who put their hope in your love.

Everything we have is because of you. I thank you for your provision for my family. I pray my children see that you are all they have and fill their hearts with gratitude.

In Jesus's name,
Amen

"Let them praise the name of the Lord, for his name alone is exalted; his splendor is above the earth and the heavens."

Psalm 148:13

BUS STOP PRAYERS

Dear God,

My children and I wake to praise you, Lord, and all of your creation. I pray my children will fall in love with you for who you are. May they feel the fullness of just *being* in your presence. Let everything they see in your glorious creation point them back to you. I pray my children and the future generations remain close to your heart, through your Son, Jesus Christ.

In his name I pray,
Amen

"For the Lord takes delight in his people; he crowns the humble with victory."

Psalm 149:4

Dear God,

How blessed we are to call you Father every morning! Make our hearts yours, guiding us to your will this day. Work inside my children to create in them a humble heart, so they may be crowned in your victory. Grow their faith that they may be called your faithful. Help me to seize every opportunity to draw them closer to you. As they lay their heads to sleep in each night, may their hearts sing your praises! May the praise of God be in their mouths and a double-edge sword in their hands. Steer their thoughts away from the enemy and keep their hearts in your hands.

In Jesus's name,
Amen

"Praise him for his acts of power; praise him for his surpassing greatness."

Psalm 150:2

Dear God,

My heart is bursting; it is so full of your love. You have brought me on this journey of intercession for my children, along with the current and future generations of children you created and have yet to create. *I know these words of the Psalms belong to you, just as our children do.* Thank you for giving us your Word as a way to know you more and as a guide to living in your perfect will. My deepest heartfelt prayer is that my children will come to know and love you and your Son. Allow our children grow to become exactly who you created them to be—working and serving for your glory. *May the words in these prayers for my children stay with them and be passed down, so your love and message of hope may be with each generation to come.*

Let everything that has breath praise the Lord Psalm 150:6 (NIV).

In Jesus's name,
Amen

About the Author

Lauren has always shared a love for children and the Lord. In addition to being a mom of three, she is delighted to bring both passions together by teaching Sunday school classes at her local church and working as an aide at God's Window Preschool.

Lauren attended James Madison University, where she met her husband, Jeremy. They currently reside in Holland, Pennsylvania with their three children, Shannon, Christopher and Tyler.